Zipolite-Beach of the Dead

MB SHELDON

Published by MB Sheldon, 2023.

ZIPOLITE-BEACH OF THE DEAD

First edition. August 4, 2023.

ISBN: 979-8223281740

Written by MB SHELDON.

Table of Contents

To my soulmate and the one true love of my life, Debra.

A Long White Winter

THE TUG ON HIS FINGER began to pull him from his dreams. For a moment he was confused about what was happening, but in the next moment he figured it out: someone was trying to steal his tent. The previous evening, he had tied one end of a piece of string to a support rod of his tent and the other end to the pointer finger of his right hand. His idea had been that the string could act like an alarm system should someone attempt to walk off with his tent in the dark of night. He really had no plan as to what he would do if that were to happen. But it was happening. He was awake now—very much awake!

Nearly Two Weeks Earlier . . .

It was April 16, 1980 and the end of the winter courses. Matthew, who was co-program director of the Breckenridge Outdoor Education Center for the Handicapped, a nonprofit organization serving clients from various counties throughout Colorado, had been anticipating this day for weeks. It had been a successful season, and the good news was that there had been no serious injuries to students or staff. But the better news was that he and his girlfriend of nearly two years, Debra, were finalizing their plans for a vacation south of the US border. They had both been silently wondering where their relationship was headed when they came up with the idea to go to Mexico. This adventure together might answer that question.

Matthew had first met Debra one afternoon while visiting a mutual friend who at that time was Debra's boyfriend. Matthew was totally captivated by the sight of Debra and thought to himself, *What a lucky guy.* There was this gorgeous redhead standing quietly behind an old couch, but the only thing he could think of to say when introduced was, "Hi." Matthew was tongue-tied. *So much for her first impression,* mused Matthew later that day.

As the months went by, Debra and Matthew would see each other here and there and occasionally have a chance to talk. Matthew, having been brought up to be respectful toward women and honor other guy's relationships with girlfriends, could only wish that Debra was his girlfriend, but he honestly had little hope that she would leave her current love for him. Little did he suspect that she had developed similar feelings for him.

In Matthew, Debra saw a gentle soul who was his own man. And so, she decided to pursue him. Being a kind person herself, she began to gently leave her boyfriend, their mutual friend. This was to be a definitive decision for Debra. She was choosing to leave a man who was making a good living in the resort community and was providing the better things in life—nice clothes, a comfortable home, the means to go out to dinner or take in a movie—for a man who was just barely getting by working odd jobs and living in what one might call "primitive conditions"—an old miner's one-room cabin sitting in an evergreen forest high up on a place called Boreas Pass at an elevation of 10,800 feet!

During the wonder years of living there as caretaker, Matthew had experienced snowfall every month of the year. There was something appealing about living like a pioneer over trying to "keep up with the Joneses." On that point both Debra and Matthew agreed, and that mutual feeling helped draw them closer together. As their shared interest in the cabin life grew and their interest in each other warmed, they began dating. Matthew had realized slowly yet steadily that he felt more at home in the mountains than any other place he had ever lived. Likewise, Debra, who was known by her friends to be a free spirit, felt at home in the woods and streams of the high country.

Throughout their courting days, they often took opportunities to go their separate ways and do their own thing. Perhaps without realizing it, they were testing the endurance of their relationship. Matthew suffered the most when they were apart, for he continued to grow fonder of the girl he thought would never be his girl. The gorgeous redhead to whom he had been so powerfully drawn those month ago was smile by smile becoming part of Matthew's being. And he loved it.

When they did spend time together, they began to speak of each other as "soul mates," which eventually became the glue that bound them together. They came to speak these words whenever they talked of how they felt about each other. Matthew was still reveling the freedom from parents, school, and military service, which all had their boundaries and were rarely in his consciousness anymore as the freedom of his daily existence left no room for such thoughts.

The concept of a soul mate had begun to register with Matthew in the early 1970s when he arrived in Breckenridge, where he had been drawn by tales of good times and freedom to make a life of one's own, as three of his brothers who preceded him to Breckenridge informed him. He was fascinated when listening and talking to his brothers, refugees from the city, who talked of living a healthier lifestyle and a balanced life of working and recreating as opposed to working fifty weeks out of the year in order to take a two-week preplanned "vacation." Ironically, as ski area employees, Matthew and Debra were doing just that—working full time, being run down for most of the six month ski season, and taking very little time off to rest and recuperate. They needed a break, a real vacation.

The idea to take a vacation to a warm climate was inspired by too many long, cold days and nights in the mountains. At the time, Debra was employed by the Breckenridge Ski Corporation as a ski instructor, and she shared a massage practice with two other local women. Matthew was co-program director of a local wilderness program for the handicapped that coordinated its winter sessions with the ski area closing date, which was always around Easter. That made it very convenient for scheduling their vacation.

The "where to go" came from Matthew's older brother Douglass, or Dougo as he was more popularly known. Dougo and a girlfriend, along with Debra and Matthew, were sharing dinner and stories one evening when Dougo started talking about the cheap plane fares, real Mexican food, and fun in the sun that he had enjoyed the previous spring. He shared stories of a place in southern Mexico, in the state of Oaxaca. Its name was Puerto Angel, and there was a nearby beach called Playa de Zipolite.

"It has warm ocean water, very clean beaches, and friendly locals. You should go check it out," he said with enthusiasm born of his personal experience.

The more Debra and Matthew listened, the more they became convinced that this Puerto Angel and its sandy beaches so far away from the snows of Breckenridge was where they had to go. This was one of those magical moments in life when one decides to do something never done before—to take a leap of faith as it were. And so, the planning began. Soon they set a date to head south—the last week of April, shortly after her job at the ski resort and his working with the outdoor education center were scheduled to end for the season.

Their plan was to carry everything they would need in backpacks. Debra had a well-worn frame pack made by Northface, and Matthew was the proud owner of a brand new, bright blue soft pack from Kelty. They chose their accessories carefully. Two of each clothing item: short-sleeved shirts, long-sleeved shirts, shorts, t-shirts, underwear, socks, handkerchiefs, etc.; but only one pair of hiking boots, sandals, sun hat, belt, sunglasses, etc. They packed paperback books, as both had developed the habit of reading just before falling asleep. They planned to carry a lightweight, three-season tent which they would split between the two of them—Matthew would carry the tent itself, and Debra would pack up the rain fly, tent pegs, and poles. Stuffed into the bottom of each pack would be three-season sleeping bags. They planned to carry water and snack foods which would consist mainly of a newly developed trail food for backpackers called "gorp" which stood for "good old raisins and peanuts." They made plans to carry traveler's checks, and they figured out a day later that visas could be picked up in Denver prior to purchasing airline tickets.

Heading South

TEN DAYS LATER THEIR journey began. They loaded their packs and themselves into the truck of a friend who was headed to Denver and was happy to give them a ride. Like most travelers, they talked excitedly about how the day would unfold but admitted that beyond this day there really was no plan. They would be dropped off at the Denver airport, fly to the Mexican border town of El Paso, Texas, catch a cab to the border crossing to Ciudad Juarez, Mexico, and walk across the border. At that point they would make their way to the train station, book tickets that included a sleeping compartment, and wake up in Mexico City. That sounded simple enough.

Early spring in Summit County meant old snow, covered with new snow, giving way to melting snow and lots of muddy streets, sidewalks, and parking lots. Springtime in the low lands meant budding trees, greening grasses, and blooming flowers. As their ride took them from the mountains of Breckenridge the white of the high country soon began to give way to the emerging green of spring on the Front Range of Colorado. Matthew's eyes began to feel the healing color of green. His sun-and-snow-blinded eyes were bathed with the many shades of green. It was natural healing at its finest. Leaving winter's constant white light to immerse himself in spring's green array of color brought such relaxation that he was tempted to close his eyes and sleep, but that would deny the welcome softer light reflecting off the snowless landscape. Besides, the excitement of the trip's beginning was too much to miss, and the green tapestry unfolding outside the truck's windshield kept drawing his eyelids back up. He would sleep that evening to the swaying of a railroad car carrying him and his girlfriend deep into Mexico.

Upon arriving in Denver, they stopped only long enough to pick up their visas, purchase their plane tickets, and board a plane run by Continental Airlines heading to El Paso, Texas. It was early in the afternoon when they landed in El Paso. Customs did not allow people to fly in or out of Mexico in the early 1980s, so they departed the twin-engine turboprop, picked up their backpacks, and got directions to the train station located across the border in Ciudad Juarez. Having done some research in the weeks before leaving Breckenridge, they knew that there was a train leaving Ciudad Juarez and headed to Mexico City that evening at 6:25 PM. All they had to do was to take a cab from the airport to the border crossing that connected El Paso, USA and Ciudad Juarez, Mexico, cross the border on foot and walk less than half a mile to the train station. Piece of cake.

Catching the Train

THEY WERE BOTH IN EXCELLENT shape and could have walked eight or ten miles had the bus depot been that far. They had plenty of time to make it to the station and purchase tickets. The train would take a full day and a half to deliver them to Mexico City. Unfortunately, they would not get to see the most spectacular scenery along the route as it would be hidden by the night.

Matthew and Debra found their sleeper car room, stowed their packs, and settled in for a brief view of the landscape before darkness overtook the light of the day. It was not long before the excitement of the adventure and the activities of the day gave way to the fact that they had been on the go since before the light of day, and soon they drifted off to the sound of the clickety-clack, clickety-clack, clickety-clack of the iron wheels of the train against the railroad tracks.

The next day began innocently enough as Matthew awoke to the gentle rocking of the train. While gazing out the sleeper car window, he said, "Buenos días, señorita. When this train stops let's find some breakfast. I'm really hungry."

"Me too," said Debra with a yawn and a gentle hands-over-the-head stretch.

As they gathered their things, they kept looking out the windows to see less and less of the Mexican countryside and more and more adobe homes, mobile homes gathered closely together, and an occasional corner market or street-side restaurant. As the train began to slow, Matthew thought to himself how he had pictured Mexico City to be much more modern than the scene outside. Shortly, the train eased to a stop, and the couple from Colorado exited into the just-awakening outskirts of the city. Grabbing their backpacks and thanking the porter for the safe ride, they exited the train and set off to look for breakfast.

Their search didn't take long since they were just looking for an authentic Mexican meal, and their noses found a place before their eyes did. The smell of warming *frijoles* caught their attention as they came upon a small cafe with a few street-side tables and chairs and the traditional *ristras*-hanging red peppers-hung from a crudely constructed awning that mostly covered the tables below. Noticing how clean the tables were, each adorned with a single marigold in a mason jar, they sat down and were soon greeted by a friendly waitress whom they found out through small talk was also the cafe owner, bus person, and hostess. She also shared the cooking and meal preparation with her husband, who was responsible for the enticing smell of cooking beans. They ordered scrambled eggs and beans with a side of corn tortillas and freshly squeezed orange juice. In no time they were served their meals, which were as they had anticipated—delicious but costing a mere seventy-five cents each. Having satisfied their hunger and feeling energized, they began walking once again toward the bus station following the directions received from the cafe owner as they paid their bill and left her a generous tip of one dollar.

It would make sense to locate both the train and bus stations near each other and, sure enough, they were. However, once they arrived at the bus station, which took much longer due to all of the gawking and sightseeing the tourists from Colorado did, they found not a single familiarly named bus line; instead there were a dozen or so independent buses more or less lined up in an open field near a one-story building that passed as the bus terminal. Each of the buses had its own distinctive paint job from front to back and top to bottom in outstanding shades of greens, oranges, reds, yellows, and purples. There were painted trees and birds and flowers and suns and sky and lots of other depictions of nature all randomly displayed. That was the way VW buses were decorated in the States, so perhaps that was where the bus owners got their inspiration. They could have named the bus line the Jungles of Mexico or Mexican Art on Wheels if they actually were all jointly owned. But as they soon found out, each bus was privately owned by proud independent drivers. Cool!

They purchased tickets and were pointed in the direction of the bus headed to their destination—Puerto Angel in the state of Oaxaca. It wasn't too hard to find, as each bus had its destination clearly advertised above their highly decorated windshields, which were partially obscured by hanging beads and tassels and multiple shaped figures. As they boarded the bus and handed the driver a handful of pesos which they had received in exchange for US dollars at the ticket window, Matthew noticed that the driver's seat was draped with a colorful sarape and a rolling beaded butt pad, the gearshift knob was a plastic nude, and the dashboard was covered with cut-to-fit pieces of thick cloth of various bold colors. Affixed to those dashboard covers were many figurines which jiggled and swayed to every movement of the bus, as Matthew later pointed out to Debra when the bus began to leave the open field. He wondered how in the world the driver could attend to the road with all that movement around the windshield, but soon he realized that all that apparent distraction was probably invisible to the driver like the frames of a pair of glasses become invisible to a person who wears them. He certainly hoped so. He wasn't eager to be involved in an accident—or any incident for that matter—on only the second day of their adventure into Mexico. A variation of this thought would recur several times in the days ahead.

The Bus Ride

DEBRA AND MATTHEW REMOVED their water bottles and a road map from their backpacks before stowing them on the metal luggage railings that ran the length of the bus above the seats. They then settled in for the long—just under nine hours—bus ride to their destination: Puerto Angel in the state of Oaxaca. Having been among the first passengers to board, they were able to get good seats on the shotgun side, second row of seats, which gave them a great view of the countryside and later the narrow, winding, unpaved road through the mountainsides. It was by design that they were among the first riders to board, as Matthew had trouble with motion sickness which was mostly eliminated if he could ride where he could see the road. Matthew had driven extensively on the old mining roads of Summit County, Colorado, therefore experiencing this ride through the mountains of southern Mexico would not be any big deal, especially since he would be able to see what the driver was seeing. It was a known fact that front seat passengers were much less prone to motion sickness than were backseat passengers because their eyes could see what ups and downs and curves were coming.

After about an hour and a half of driving through the countryside on mostly paved roadways, the bus started to climb into the mountains, and it was then that they transitioned from paved road to dirt road and from straight to winding. It was a short time later that Matthew realized that their driver was quite skilled at handling the bus; he felt that he and Debra were in good hands. As their eyes met he mentioned his confidence in the driver's skill and she said she felt the same way.

Matthew could sense her confidence even before speaking to her as the bus moved rapidly past precipitous drop-offs that fell steeply into the jungled valleys below. There was an acknowledgement of the thrill of the ride expressed by a shared widening of the eyes coupled with tight-lipped smiles. They weren't scared, for years of doing the same sort of narrow-dirt-and-gravel mountain driving themselves smoothed their nerves and brought a sense of trust for their obviously skilled mountain roads driver.

The bus came around a bend in the road and began to slow. Ahead they could see what appeared to be a group of people in the roadway and one was holding up a hand with the palm facing forward—the universal sign to stop. It turned out to be a soldier brandishing an automatic rifle and a sidearm, and there were some other soldiers also standing in the road behind the soldier signaling the bus to stop. He did not signal the bus driver to pull over but rather to stop in the road. Debra and Matthew exchanged looks of wonder and mild concern as the bus came to a halt. The driver, obviously used to this, came to a stop, shut off the engine, and snapped open the bus door.

Several thoughts raced into Matthew's mind while he tried to figure out what was happening. Were these soldiers stopping them to warn them of a natural disaster ahead or was the bus driver in cahoots with these guys dressed up as soldiers to rob the passengers? The weather was fine and there had been no signs of even a little rain, so he quickly ruled out a rock slide or a washed-out road. If this was a setup for robbery, then they had badly miscalculated who was sharing that bus ride south. There were only peasants, young children, and two tourists from Colorado with next to no cash in their possession. No, there had to be another explanation, but right away it became obvious that the situation was serious. The three soldiers armed with M16s purposefully boarded the bus as the leader was issuing orders in Spanish. One remained at the front of the bus where there were only a few empty seats while the other two moved swiftly to the middle and back of the bus. By then Matthew had figured out that they were looking for someone or something.

Despite their different cultural backgrounds, the two Americans reacted the same as the Mexican passengers—they basically froze and dared not move. A hush fell over the passengers. Matthew, who occupied an aisle seat, began to listen to what was happening behind them. He still could not figure out whether they were looking for someone or something. He dared not turn around but did turn his head slightly to catch Debra's eyes which by then showed deep concern. He turned his eyes to the back of the seat in front of him, then shot a glance to the soldier standing at the front of the bus in "port arms" position. He was all business.

Part of Matthew's growing apprehension stemmed from the fact that he knew about the weapons that these soldiers were carrying, for he had been in the Army ten years previously and had intimate knowledge of how powerful and deadly they were. In particular, he recalled firing the same .45-caliber handgun each soldier was carrying. He remembered how loud they were when discharged, but more vividly he recalled the "kick" as the gun fired and how uncontrollable it felt in his hands. Those thoughts flashed in his memory in an instant as he glanced away from the soldier in front and back to Debra to again face the back of the seat in front of him.

Then the search came to Matthew. They weren't looking for anyone—they were searching bags and packs. They were probably looking for drugs! He could now hear one of the soldiers moving nearer to him. With a slight turn of his head he could barely see but mostly sense that the soldier was only a couple of seats behind where he and Debra were sitting and that he had released his non-trigger-finger hand from his rifle and was checking bags in the luggage rack above the seats on the driver's side of the bus. His back was turned to Matthew and Debra as he went about poking and prodding. At that moment

Debra leaned closer to Matthew and mouthed, "You don't have any pot, do you?"

Matthew's lips pulled back slightly exposing just a portion of his front teeth, and his tongue moved forward to touch the back of his lower front teeth as his mouth prepared to make the "Y" sound. As Debra had done to him, he only mouthed the word "Yes" back to her. If looks could kill, the one that Debra flashed at Matthew would have ended his life then and there. He knew that she was both extremely angry and extremely frightened at the same time.

He hadn't even given a thought, up until that moment, to the possible consequences of carrying marijuana across the border into a foreign country, because he had been freely carrying it around in his home state of Colorado for years without incident. Yeah, it was illegal to possess at that time, but as long as you weren't distributing it, nobody cared. Now the problem was that they both knew he had weed in his backpack. Debra and Matthew slipped silently into private panic. Matthew's hands, already folded in his lap, opened ever so slowly allowing the thumb and first finger of his right hand to slide to the meaty part of the left hand and begin massaging the muscles and soft tissue below the skin. This was a technique used to promote overall body relaxation that he had learned in previous years studying and practicing massage. Adding in some imperceptible deep breaths, he began to try to alleviate a growing sense of panic. He noticed that Debra had begun to use the same techniques, for she too had studied massage and was a full-time practitioner back home in Breckenridge, Colorado.

ZZZZZZZZZZZIP went the zipper on his brand new Kelty backpack, followed by the sound of a plastic bag being pulled through the small side-pocket opening. Matthew's heart rate started to rise, and he felt blood rushing to his head and making his face flush with color—or was it suddenly draining from his head making him look whiter and paler than normal? He wasn't sure. He just knew that the soldier with the huge rifle was now standing next to him, barely inches away. His left brown-skinned hand held the weapon close to his body while the weight of the rifle was supported by an OD—olive drab—strap. That allowed him to use his right hand to freely rifle through the passenger's belongings, including Matthew's own.

Oh shit! he thought as panic began to set in. The soldier was pulling the pot out of Matthew's bright, sky-blue backpack. Matthew's face was flushed with color, and beads of sweat began to drip from his armpits. *Why that pocket?* he cursed silently. *Of all the possible pockets and other openings that the backpack has to offer, why that particular one?* But then the soldier stopped handling the plastic bag and turned to check a bag made of cloth sitting on the steel rack on the opposite side of the aisle. Matthew took a long, slow, deep breath as nonchalantly as he could and then exhaled just as slowly with tentative relief. In what seemed like only seconds, but in reality had been minutes later, the soldier in charge shouted, "Vámanos," and the soldiers departed the bus. The bus driver restarted the engine and snapped the doors shut. While looking in the large overhead rearview mirror to see that everyone was still seated, he drove off.

Now Matthew and Debra were free to move their bodies, which had been nearly motionless ever since the soldiers had first stepped onto the bus. As he moved his head from side to side, first giving Debra a sheepish look then turning back to the left and catching a glimpse of the plastic bag now hanging out of his backpack for all to see, one overriding question sprang to his mind. Why had the soldier stopped pulling the bag out of his pack? Did the soldier not really believe in his government's mission to try to stop the smuggling of illegal drugs and was just going through the motions of trying to find them, or did he suddenly take pity on these two foreigners—or what? The reason really did not matter. Matthew realized at that moment that something extraordinary had just happened, and what could have turned into a terrible situation suddenly became just a part of the early hours of what was to become an extraordinary adventure.

Then Debra started to angrily whisper to Matthew, "What in the hell were you thinking? Why are you carrying pot? Do you not understand that this is not the United States, not Breckenridge, Colorado, anymore? Why didn't you tell me or at least ask me if we ought to take some pot on our trip? Are you crazy?"

She really let him have it for a minute or so. Matthew could only hunch his shoulders and say, "Sorry."

No, he really hadn't given the implications of carrying marijuana into a foreign country any thought. What he had thought was that there might be some time along the way when they could get high. She gave him that if-looks-could-kill look again, continued to fume, and turned to look out the window of the now accelerating bus. Perhaps the driver was attempting to make up for lost time, although they only then began to wonder if the bus driver really concerned himself with the schedule and if the bus would arrive in Puerto Angel within nine hours according to the schedule they had noticed when they had bought their tickets. Matthew and Debra hadn't given it much thought. Why should they? They were on an adventure.

A half hour, perhaps an hour passed by as the thoughts and images of the search filled their heads along with the possible implications if things had gone differently. Matthew continued to wonder about why the soldier had suddenly stopped pulling the bag out of his pack and how things might have gone had he yanked it out into full view exposing his stash of marijuana which was contained in a leather hip pouch held shut by a roach clip. The clip was actually a device known to electricians as an "alligator clip," which was and still is used for creating a temporary electrical connection. Many pot smokers found that they were very useful for holding on to the very end of a joint that was still burning but too short or too hot for handling. *It must be fate intervening*, he thought. He and Debra were destined to continue their journey on to some other conclusion. It wasn't going to end on that second day with them being locked up in a jail in some small Mexican town where they would be pleading for their rights to, at a minimum, make a phone call. No, he thought, this incident was just a bump in the road or perhaps a warning to pay more attention to what was going on around them. Or something else. He just didn't have the answer, so he began to let those thoughts go and focus on the bus ride as once again it sped through the mountainous terrain of southern Mexico.

The bus popped out of the jungle into a clearing exposing a small village, and as they came closer, they could see a dozen or so men, women, and children standing alongside the dirt road. The bus slowed and came to a full stop. Matthew was surprised that the bus was taking on more passengers, but why should he be surprised? That was what buses did.

This time the bus driver pulled on the door lever and gently opened the double doors. With a customary "Hola," the driver welcomed the villagers to climb aboard his transport. This instantly began to settle Matthew's apprehension, which quickly changed to curiosity as the new passengers filed onto the bus. There were about a dozen or so adults—men wearing well-worn shirts and faded pants with even more timeworn sandals, women with more colorful over-the-knee-length dresses, some skillfully embroidered in an array of brightly colored designs. There were children dressed similarly to the adults who accompanied them, but what stood out most prominently was how clean looking they all were. And their hair—the shorter cuts on the men and boys and the long shiny black hair of the younger girls and the older women—shown brilliantly in the near midday light. They were a handsome people. Their confidence was evident, as many of them made eye contact with Matthew and Debra, some briefly, others with a smile and a nod of the head. One young girl of 10, perhaps 11 or 12, moved past Matthew and Debra with her arms cradling a chicken! How startling and amusing. Then shortly thereafter came a teenage boy leading a small pig by a rope leash. *Wow*, thought Matthew, *I've never seen that before.*

The doors of the bus clapped shut, and the bus's engine once again began to work its way smoothly up through the gears. As there had been no empty seats remaining, all of the new passengers held on either with a reach above to the luggage rack or to the edge of the nearest seat. Just as he remembered his upbringing had taught him to be a gentleman and offer up his seat, Debra said, "Let's give that woman"—with a baby in her arms and a small child holding on to her skirt— "our seats." And so, they did. They stood up, maneuvered their way out of the seats, and gestured with their arms and open hands toward their seats. She gave the Coloradoans a warm, understanding smile and accepted the seats.

Now they were standing with the rest of the village people, and what immediately caught Matthew's attention was that he was experiencing something for the first time in his life. As he casually looked around, he realized that he, at only 5' 8", was the tallest person standing in the aisle of the bus.

The bus hummed along, automatically downshifting and upshifting as the road dictated the pace. They were standing mostly side by side holding on to the overhead rack, shifting arms as they tired of holding one above their heads, sometimes gripping the edge of a nearby seat, then back to the overhead rack especially as the bus driver negotiated sharp curves because it was easier on the hands and wrists to hold on above. All the shifting and changing of body position gave the couple the advantage of seeing each other from many angles. No matter how he looked at her, Matthew sometimes got lost in her beauty. He didn't mind the standing as the constant rock and roll of the bus forced him and Debra to continually bump or lean into each other as they talked about this and that or simply gazed out the passenger windows or shared the view the driver saw through the windshield. He loved being with her, next to her. It was a thrilling ride for sure.

It was a good thing that Debra and Matthew had strong legs developed by spending so many hours hiking and skiing during the years prior to taking their adventure to the southern reaches of Mexico, because the bus ride just kept going and going without stopping until after many hours it pulled off the dirt road in a tiny village that was mostly in the shade of the jungle-like canopy. Within moments there appeared children, maybe as many as eight or ten, carrying food and drinks: bananas and mangos and, curiously, 7-Ups and Cokes. Some of them moved to the door of the bus, which was just opening, but most came right up to the side of the bus and started to hawk their wares to the passengers still seated next to the windows.

"Coke, señorita? Banana, señor?" said one entrepreneur while holding up glass bottles of the popular drinks.

"Yo tengo Chiclets," said another.

Since they had had no bathroom break up to this point and they had been sipping water, their immediate concern was to find a bathroom. They tentatively got off the bus, and while politely declining the many offers from the children, they spotted an older man. Debra, who knew a fair amount of conversational Spanish, asked, "Dónde está el baño?" The man pointed the way, and they quickly found the one and only toilet. So, Matthew "stood guard" as Debra went first, and then they switched, keeping a keen eye out for the bus driver, not wishing to be left high and dry in the village. They finished their business and, again declining the many offers of food and drink, reboarded the still waiting bus. They were indeed relieved in more than one way.

Puerto Angel

IT WOULD BE YET ANOTHER three and a half hours before they reached their destination: Puerto Angel. Puerto Angel was a small coastal town located almost due west of the city of Oaxaca on the Pacific Ocean side of southern Mexico. Originally a hub for the region's coffee and lumber industries, it was now more of a community of fishermen with a sprinkle of tourism development. Although they didn't think of themselves as tourists but rather as adventure seekers, they were indeed visiting for pleasure. As the bus pulled into town and came to a stop near a cluster of shacks and cabanas, the sun was well on its way toward sinking into the watery horizon to the west. It would be dark in a couple of hours, so the two adventure seekers each privately were thinking about where they were going to spend the night. Matthew waited for the majority of passengers, including the pig and the chicken, to move toward the exit before he pulled their packs from the overhead rack, handed the older looking one to Debra, and slipped one shoulder strap of his new backpack over his shoulder, being mindful of the other passengers about him, and he and Debra exited the bus.

Scanning their surroundings, they soon realized that what they saw was nowhere near what even Cuidad Juarez had to offer. There were no streets, no restaurants, no motels, no markets, no nothing aside from a few run-down one-story buildings, a rickety boardwalk leading out into the bay, and a handful of cabanas, some with wooden tables and wicker chairs.

"Got any ideas?" Debra asked as she took in the laid-back village by the sea.

"Yeah. First let's find el baño. I've been holding it for quite a while." Debra agreed with both statements.

The second local that they asked, "Dónde es el baño?" pointed to a small concrete structure with no door. Debra encouraged Matthew to go first; she would "stand guard" at the entrance. Matthew entered the bathroom with expectations of at least a toilet and a sink but was amazed to find nothing but an empty room with a hole in the center of the floor. *Interesting*, he thought. It was a good thing that he had a boy scout mentality and was always prepared as he pulled some toilet paper from his pack. The couple from Colorado exchanged places as Matthew handed off his small roll of toilet paper and stood in front of the door hoping no one, especially any male, would suddenly need the bathroom. He washed his hands with some undisturbed sand, as did Debra when she shortly emerged. Then they began to search for a room for the night.

They hadn't gone very far when a local spotted them and gave them a warm "Hola, mis amigos" and an even warmer ear to ear smile. He might as well have been a local version of a chamber of commerce greeter as he began to speak to the travelers in quite good English, asking if they were looking for a place to stay. Was it that obvious, they wondered? They replied that they were and asked if he could direct them to an inexpensive motel. He laughed and told them not to bother looking, for there were none, but they would be more than welcome to stay right there under the thatched roof of his cabana with him and his family. Having come prepared to camp out, Debra and Matthew looked at each other, agreed that they felt comfortable accepting the congenial Mexican's offer, especially seeing the man's family smiling or grinning at them, and said, "Si. Muchas gracias."

Right away they were offered some bottled water and beer, but they quickly realized that they were quite exhausted from the day's adventure and accepted the water only. They drank the bottled water and answered the usual questions one asks a stranger: "Where are you from?", "What's your name?", and "Where are you headed?" As they chatted they noticed the darkening skies and feeling the warm summer breeze sliding in off the bay became aware of how tired they were and politely excused themselves from the man and his companions, pulled out their sleeping pads and bags, spread them not far from the table and chairs where their host sat drinking cerveza with his adult family members, and soon fell into an exhausted sleep.

Day three of their adventure found Debra and Matthew awakening to the early morning light of the fishing community of Puerto Angel tucked in along the Pacific Ocean side of the southern coast of Mexico. Someone was stirring about as they regained their bearings and realized that it was their friendly host who was at the moment encouraging a small smoky fire with little pieces of driftwood.

"Buenos días, amigos," said one of their host's friends who turned out to be a Marine who was off duty and was along with his buddies having a jolly time and making the most of their short leave. "Cerveza?"

Now, the two adventurers had certainly had a beer before midday before, and Matthew remembered trying to cure a hangover with a beer for breakfast in the not too distant past; however, being offered a beer upon awakening—not even out of bed, or bag as it were—was certainly a first.

"Uh, no thanks. Maybe later," fumbled Matthew.

As they got up and shook the sand from their sleeping bags before stuffing them back into their stuff-sacks, Matthew and Debra were amused by the fact that the Marines were already quite jovial, as they had started in on their beer drinking some time before, or were perhaps just carrying on from the night before. It wasn't clear which scene was true, but what was true was that they were respectful fellows in their drunken state, as they had not been so rowdy throughout the night or during the early morning as to have disturbed the sleeping couple.

Since the previous day had been such a long and eventful one, including the highly emotional drug search by the soldiers and the fact that they had stood for nearly all of the nine-hour bus ride, they could not turn down the next offer, which was for a hot breakfast of scrambled eggs, cooked beans, and warm tortillas. They ate heartily while answering a new round of questions. Their host offered some Coronas, and this time they accepted. It was a nice compliment to the breakfast meal, which one could expect since the combination of Mexican food and beer had been enjoyed by diners all over the world for perhaps a century or more. The only difference now was that it was morning, not even nine o'clock. Matthew and Debra finished their meal and tried to pay, but their money was refused. So, they thanked their host twice again and set off walking to their ultimate destination—Zipolite. Having found out that it was only about a mile away, they made their way along a dirt road feeling slightly high from the beer, but strong in the legs as they were still in top notch condition from the just ended ski season, not to mention that they were now at sea level having dropped down from nearly 11,000 feet. Breathing was so easy that morning.

Talking and reminiscing as they walked, they soon came to a small village that had an open area filled with vendors. It was the beach community of Playa de Zipolite, and they had come upon an open market that was filled with activity and vibrant chatter. As they wandered about checking out the various vendor stands, not looking for anything in particular, they began to notice that they were the object of curious onlooking men, women, and children, many of whom came up to them offering what seemed to be freshly made breads as well as the now familiar Cokes and Chiclets. Having eaten not long before, it was easy to say, "No, gracias," even though there was a twinge of pity for the children who were just trying to help support their families by selling stuff to the tourists. It didn't occur to the American tourists until later that those children were under the watchful eyes of their parents standing not too far away in the crowd. As it turned out, those concerned parents were not the only ones watching the tourists from Colorado.

There were colorful shirts and skirts and sun hats and sombreros along with interesting seashells being offered individually as well as neatly strung together to make nice looking necklaces. "No, gracias" continued to be their response as Matthew and Debra wandered about the open market under the clear blue sky with the hint of moisture in the air. They both realized that anything they bought, no matter how neat or cool, would only add to the weight of their backpacks; plus they had to watch closely how much money they spent, as they only had a vague idea of how much they would need for the rest of their vacation. The one expenditure that they were sure of was the return flight out of Mexico, for they had purchased round-trip tickets at the beginning of their adventure. Every friend back home in Colorado that they had talked with about the idea of traveling out of country had given the same advice: when purchasing tickets, make them round-trip tickets so that in case they were to run short of money or worse lost their money, at least they could still get a plane ride home as long as they didn't lose their tickets too. That thought—losing their tickets—was not in their minds as they continued their buzzed walk through Playa de Zipolite.

It was now late morning, and the combined effects of the heat and the sun and the beers for breakfast were all conspiring to make it hard to continue on, so the two soul mates went looking for the ocean, a cold drink, and some shade. They were ready to just hang out.

In a matter of minutes, they came upon a well-built cabana with inviting shade and a small bar set safely back from the rolling waves of the great Pacific Ocean. As soon as they entered the shade of the thatched roof structure, they knew they had found what they had been looking for ever since their conversations with Matthew's brother Dougo began to pique their interest in going on a vacation to find warmth and relaxation. They literally dropped into some seats and ordered a couple of Coronas. It was time to melt into the beach and the sounds of the ocean waves. "Ahhhhhhhhh," they sighed in unison. "This is the life," proclaimed Matthew, lifting his bottle of Corona while offering a toast to Debra. She tapped her bottle to his with a huge smile and a resounding, "Yes. Here's to the good life."

In the 1970s there was a restlessness and an awakening of the spirit of adventure among younger men and women who earned the title of "hippies." They were "hip," or aware of all things new and old at the same time. They left their homes and went looking for new adventurers in faraway places, and Playa de Zipolite was one such place.

It was barely midday as Matthew and Debra settled into a couple of wooden chairs with thick cushions nestled under the swaying palm leaves that made up the roof of the ocean-side cabana. At first, they talked about how wonderful it felt to be so relaxed and warm and free to do whatever they pleased, as opposed to just five short days before when they were pushing themselves out of bed to a 26 degree morning in Breckenridge, Colorado, putting on the necessary layers of polypropylene underwear, lined pants, long-sleeved turtlenecks, sweaters, hats, coats, insulated boots with Vibram soles, and finally some insulated gloves just to go outside and warm up the car before heading off to their last day of work at the ski area.

Matthew idly pushed his toes into the warm tan colored beach sand and felt the cooler sand below the surface before raising his foot up out of the sand, spreading his toes, and watching as the dryer grains of sand filtered and fell back to the beach floor in the shade of his, for the time being, favorite place in the whole world. He repeated that sand-diving–coming-up-for-air motion over and over, spreading his toes ever so slightly wider each time, and finally realizing that this is what his ski-boot-confined toes had been craving for so many months. As he and Debra continued to sip their drinks and reminisce, he noticed that she was also sand-dipping her toes in just the same manner. Muscle tension was melting away.

Matthew pulled his ball cap down further to create more shade as he continued to talk and listen to Debra while becoming more conscious of the mesmerizing waves rolling in and out. His eyelids began to drop lower and lower. Debra had stopped talking and she too was slipping deeper into her cushioned wicker chair.

"Whoa," said Debra as she shook her head from side to side and blinked her eyes as wide open as she could in the sunlight of the day. "I'm falling asleep. I've got to get up and move around. Let's go check out the beach."

Matthew took a deep breath and convincing himself that she was right pushed himself out of his seat, paid for their drinks, tipped their server, and hoisted his pack up and over his shoulder. It seemed heavier than before he had sat down. The events of the previous days combined with the drinks and newfound warmth began melting the two adventurers like two pats of butter on a warm skillet. They walked slowly, almost aimlessly, figuring that eventually they would snap out of their semiconscious state of mind. It was such a lovely feeling as their cares slipped away with each sandy step. Better, much better.

They continued to wander and talk as subconsciously they took in the sight and sound of the waves sometimes rolling in and occasionally slapping the already damp sand of the shore line. They stopped briefly to remove their sandals and then continued their stroll veering closer to the ocean's beckoning blue-green water. Now each footstep left a deeper imprint in the smooth, wet canvas of the shoreline. Their pace slowed so that they could savor the feeling and vision of each step luxuriating in the warm surface sand oozing upward between their toes that had been confined in ski boots and mostly cold for so many months. This warm touch of the surface sand was quickly replaced by the contrasting chill of the sand beneath the warmer sand on top followed by the even cooler splash of the waves of ocean saltwater. Although the water was only ankle deep, it was enough to inform them of the temperature of the water, which was most inviting compared to the mountain lakes they occasionally jumped into back home. In fact, it was refreshingly cool, as the sand was by that time of the day starting to be too hot to the touch of their tender feet.

The afternoon passed slowly but surely as the two lovers walked and talked now and then, holding hands and occasionally venturing further out into the surf, but eventually the skibums-turned-beachbums made their way back toward the cabana where they had started their afternoon and grabbed a light hunger-satisfying meal while they began to figure out where they were going to sleep that night. Their beach walk had been a long one, and the shadows of the evening made them aware of how the day had slipped away.

Ignoring Good Advice

IT WAS 1980 AND THERE were no laws forbidding sleeping on the beach in Zipolite, Mexico, and although the two adventurers had been advised by their host the previous night that it might be safer (there was mention of tourists being robbed) to pay a few pesos and sleep under a cabana, they chose to camp on a high spot of the beach less than a quarter mile from Zipolite village. They were, after all, veteran campers who were used to hiking and camping just about anywhere they chose in the national forests of Colorado. They always sought out isolated sites that allowed them to enjoy the scenery and solitude during the day and the stars and peacefulness of the night.

After a short discussion about whether to set up the tent in case it rained or just roll out their three-season sleeping bags and pads, Debra and Matthew decided to sleep under the stars. The weather was balmy with a gentle breeze and some high cumulonimbus clouds.

With the light of day fading away, they sat down in the sand to watch and listen to the waves lap upon the sandy shoreline, which by now had receded a safe distance away. It was time to take in the sunset while gazing westward over the great Pacific Ocean. Matthew realized, at that moment perhaps for the first time, that one of the things that he appreciated about Debra was how she didn't feel the need to talk when she was with him. Silence was totally acceptable. He would come to find out later that that was true for her also. They loved just being with one another.

The sky on the far horizon was turning a soft salmon color with some of the flatter-bottomed clouds taking on a slightly deeper tone of red making for a so-so sunset. It didn't matter. It was a perfect setting and a perfect ending to a day they had both been looking forward to for months. As the sun sank out of the faint pink and darkening sky and past the horizon, the two pleasantly weary travelers, realizing how exhausted they truly were, turned to one another, kissed, and rising from their sitting positions, spanked the dry but somewhat sticky sand from their shorts and legs, and crawled into their sleeping bags by the sea. Matthew had chosen to sleep naked, but Debra opted to sleep in her bathing suit. The evening breeze had just a hint of coolness to prompt them both to unzip their sleeping bags, flip the top back over their bodies, but leave their feet sticking out. But, just before dozing off, Debra spotted lightning in the distance; so they got back out of their sleeping bags and set up the tent near where their pads and bags lay. Now they were ready in case some rain was to sweep over the ocean. After shoving their backpacks into the tent they got back in their bags, watched the distant lightning perform its wonderous light show against the clouds until they could no longer keep their eyes open, and fell into a deep sleep.

The tug on his finger began to pull him from his dreams. For a moment he was confused about what was happening, but in the next moment he figured it out: someone was trying to steal his tent. The previous evening, he had tied one end of a piece of string to a support rod of his tent and the other end to the pointer finger of his right hand. His idea had been that the string could act like an alarm system should someone attempt to walk off with his tent in the dark of night. He really had no plan as to what he would do if that were to happen. But it was happening. He was awake now—very much awake!

Suddenly, there were shadowy figures surrounding them shouting, "*Dinero*!! *Dinero*!!" Matthew and Debra knew enough Spanish to understand what it was that the strangers were yelling. "Money." They wanted *their* money.

Without thinking, but simply reacting, the two adventurers sprang to their feet as the human instinct to fight or run sent a surge of adrenaline coursing throughout their bodies. Matthew chose to fight, as he had done many times in his life because he had always thought of himself as being bigger and stronger than his actual body size. In reality he was only five feet eight inches tall and weighed just 136 pounds. During a football game in high school as a ball carrier, he had once faced an immense defensive lineman who stood between him and the goal line, and Matthew had decided rather foolishly to try and run through him. The kid was almost as wide as he was tall. Whack! It was like running into a wall, as Matthew was bounced backwards and sent sprawling to the field barely holding onto the ball.

"Dinero!! Dinero!!" he heard again. Then came a blow to his upper left arm. Wow, that hurt! What was that?? Whack! Another blow struck him on his right forearm. Whack! Yet another struck him on his chest. Now his eyes were wide open and fully adjusted to the darkness. He then saw that these robbers were wielding machetes!!

Meanwhile Debra was putting up her own fight, kicking and slapping her assailants as she too had been raised to defend herself; but even more to the point, she was a feisty redhead. She had learned early on to fight back. In high school in Denver, Colorado, during the forced integration of the early 1970s, she had been cornered in the girls' bathroom of George Washington High School by a group of black girls and had put up quite the resistance until an unlikely ally—another black girl who saw the injustice of five against one—stepped in to save her. Now, however, she was on her own taking swings at her assailants and yelling and generally making quite a commotion which, as it turned out, was a saving grace. To get her to settle down one of the robbers grabbed ahold of her red hair, which she had pulled into a pony tail before laying down that night, and yanked her head backwards—which only angered her even more. She screamed and attempted to turn and hit her attacker when—Whack! —she too received an attention-getting blow on her back from the flat of a machete. That quieted her right down.

Matthew was getting the picture more slowly. Determined not to give up their money, he went to the tent where he and Debra had stashed their backpacks and reached blindly into the center portion of his backpack. Turning his head back towards the tent entrance, he yelled, "I'll get the gun! I'll get the gun!"

Apparently, the robbers didn't understand English, or they were now worried that Debra's noisy resistance may have been heard by the locals, or both, one of them simply grabbed Matthew's backpack and forcefully yanked it out of the tent. Matthew was still determined to resist and turned on his knees and latched onto it with both hands. Whack! That blow did the trick, for the assailants now had Matthew's full, but stunned attention. They had struck him forcefully on the top of his head. He let go of his pack and sank onto his haunches, his arms hanging limp at his sides and his head bowed in submission. Everything became quiet as the robbers disappeared with his backpack into the night.

After a few moments Matthew heard a somewhat faraway voice ask, "Are you okay?" It was Debra. "Are you hurt?" she investigated. At first, Matthew couldn't be sure if he was alright and didn't know how to answer. Then he felt something warm sliding down the side of his face. He reached up and touched the side of his head just behind his right eye with the fingers of his right hand. It was his own blood.

It was sometime after midnight, and it was still dark. Matthew sat slumped upon his heels which pushed his toes inches into the now cool sands of the beach at Zipolite. He was stunned and bleeding from his several wounds and starting to go into shock. Debra was unhurt, but she was alarmed and fearful.

Off in the distance dogs were barking, but neither Matthew nor Debra heard them.

Matthew was finally able to speak and forced out a weak, "I'm okay." But he really didn't mean it. His mind flashed back to a moment in 1964 during a high school football game when he had been momentarily knocked out. His dad, who was the team doctor—a practicing neurosurgeon no less—asked the question, "Are you alright?" Matthew responded with a feeble, "Yes," because he so loved to play football and did not want to come out of the game even though he knew he was not alright. He could hardly stand up, let alone walk without assistance to the sideline.

Debra quickly went to the tent and withdrew her backpack, which the robbers had fortunately left untouched, and searched for and found a handkerchief, which she then placed on Matthew's head and told him to hold in place. With some effort he did so while Debra then searched for and found a small flashlight in a side pocket of her pack.

"We've got to get you to a doctor," she said.

"Un huh," mumbled Matthew, whose head was starting to ache. But of more concern was that he was getting drowsy. Debra sensed all of what was going on with Matthew but urged him to stand up, for they needed to pack up their tent and get Matthew to some help. As he forced himself up, it was then that Debra realized that Matthew was not dressed to start walking to see anyone. He was naked.

It was not unusual for him to go to bed wearing nothing, for he had done it for years while living as a caretaker in a cabin which sat at 10,800 feet some five miles south of Breckenridge, Colorado, where the temperature often got well below zero in December and January. He claimed that he slept better that way with layers of blankets and his body's own internal heater to keep him warm. He had also devised a plan whereby he would place a clean set of underwear and an undershirt under the covers with him so that they would be warm for the mornig and he could slip them on after waking before throwing back the covers and hastily getting fully dressed. But this time he had no such clothes, not even underwear. All his clothes had disappeared with the thieves into the night. Fortunately, he and Debra were nearly the same size, and she gave him a pair of shorts and a t-shirt to wear. As she steadied him and he clumsily began to dress, he began to feel faint and asked her to let him sit back down in the sand. But she rejected his request saying, "Oh no you don't! You are not going to pass out now. No way! I'll get the tent, and then we need to go find some help."

And so, she wadded up the tent, stuffed the sleeping bags into their stuff-sacks, and hastily rolled up the pads before handing them to Matthew. Then she forced him to begin walking. With great effort and with Debra's constant urging, he shuffled along the beach holding her handkerchief on the top of his head, from which the blood had ceased flowing, while carrying the two pads in the opposite arm. They kept moving toward some lights in the village of Zipolite until they stumbled upon a group of Mexican students in a beach-side cabana who were still up, apparently winding down from some late-night partying. When Debra asked for their help, she was relieved to find that they spoke English. The students immediately recognized the situation, and two of them guided Matthew and Debra toward the town constable's house.

As they got to the edge of the community, the students pointed out the constable's house and then departed. It was only then that Debra, and to a much lesser extent Matthew, became aware of all the barking dogs.

Debra knocked urgently on the door, noticing that some house lights were already on. The door was jerked open by the constable who simply said, "Si?"

As Debra and Matthew stepped into the light that sprang from the doorway, it was obvious what they needed. The local lawman and his wife who by then had come up next to the constable could plainly see the condition Matthew was in. He had dried blood stains from the top of his head, down the side of his face, curling under his jaw and down his neck, and leading to the partially blood-stained t-shirt which he had borrowed from Debra. No words from Debra were necessary, as it was obvious to the Mexican couple what they needed to do.

"Entran, entran," said the woman as she and her partner moved out of the doorway and ushered the strangers into their home. Debra and now the wife of the constable supported Matthew and eased him into a solidly built wooden chair which the constable had pulled out from under an equally solid wooden table as he motioned for Matthew to sit down. Even though he was in a state of shock, Matthew who was raised to be respectful of others, especially adults, thanked them all with a feeble "Gracias." Then the constable's wife began to tend to Matthew's head wound, and Debra began to explain what had happened on the beach. However, it quickly became apparent that the woman did not understand any English. Holding up the pointer finger of her right hand and looking directly at Debra, she displayed the universal gesture meaning "Hold on," as she turned to her man and said, "Ve por el chico de Gloria." He went out the door into the night. Debra told Matthew that she thought it meant that the constable was sent to get someone named Gloria. Actually the constable was sent to find Gloria's son.

Then the small Mexican woman filled a brightly decorated clay bowl with tap water and, using a clean cloth, began to clean up Matthew's major wound and the trail of blood it had produced. It was then that Debra first noticed that Matthew had other superficial wounds on his left arm, one on the forearm and one on the biceps. Then Matthew realized that he had other wounds that began to call for his attention. He reached for the hem of the borrowed t-shirt and lifted it up to reveal a long, clean cut on the right side of his chest. Fortunately, it was only a surface wound and had bled only slightly. Between the three of them—Matthew, Debra, and the small Mexican woman—they carefully removed the shirt to inspect for further injury. In a later conversation with Debra as she and Matthew recalled this scene, Matthew, an EMT, would remark that it had been a great example of well-done triage—the careful assessment of someone with known and unknown injuries.

As the woman of the house and Debra were tending to Matthew's wounds, the husband reappeared with a younger man who turned out to be the son of the owner of a local seaside resort.

"Hello," he said in English. "My name is Mario. It looks like you have had a rough night." Turning to Debra he added, "So what happened?"

The little woman had found some first aid pads and was applying one to Matthew's head and securing it with some household tape. Debra began again to explain things, and as she did so Mario began to translate. Debra, who knew a bit of conversational Spanish, began to detail the events of the previous hour with the young man adding what Spanish words and phrases that she could recall. The constable, who had been taking notes on a small spiral notebook, soon entered into the conversation and quickly became irritated. Mario translated into English what was upsetting him.

Meanwhile Matthew shifted himself in the mildly comfortable wooden chair and began to look around the room in his dazed and slightly confused condition. He tried with great effort to listen to the conversation.

Mario explained that his mother as well as many of the residents of their small ocean-side village had for a number of years been collectively trying to build up tourism as a way to survive because the previous sustaining commerce of the area—logging and the exportation of coffee—had almost died out. Incidents of robbery were particularly upsetting to the constable and his wife, who struggled to make ends meet as he worked part-time as a dock worker and she helped a friend sell handmade necklaces and earrings at the village market. They then asked Debra if she and Matthew would be willing to file a report. Debra caught Matthew's distant attention, and he said in a subdued but supportive voice, "Sure."

Mario added his and his mothers' concerns to the conversation about the village's honest attempt to change their economy and bemoaned this incident as a setback.

Debra and Matthew were to find out in the days that followed that they were not the first tourists to be victimized by robbers. It had been a rough couple of years for the local fishermen, dock workers, loggers, and coffee industry workers as a whole, and the community had suffered the added embarrassment of more and more robberies. But this incident that involved robbery *and* assault was not going to set well when the word got out into the community.

"I believe a lot of the community already knows something bad just happened," said the constable's wife in Spanish. "My husband and I were awakened by all the barking dogs, so I am sure there are many others who are aware that something bad has happened. This happens too often. Many dogs start barking when there is trouble."

Matthew asked for some water and the constable's wife went to her kitchen sink and grabbed a crudely made mug with finely painted flowers showing the stamens and pistils in brilliant reds, yellows, and greens. She then filled it with water from a pitcher which she pulled from her refrigerator. "Not too much," cautioned Debra, remembering her first aid that taught that if there is a suspected head injury to give no or very little liquid to the victim. Matthew acknowledged her warning with an "Uh huh," also remembering the same guidelines from his first aid and EMT trainings.

Matthew had taken the emergency medical training in order to become a backcountry guide. It was something he had wanted to be ever since completing his NOLS (National Outdoor Leadership School) instructor's course in the mid-1970s. He did get to co-lead a 32-day NOLS course the following summer into the North Cascades of Washington State, which both cemented his love for hiking and camping in the wilderness and also gave him a reality check to just how much weight his small body could carry. During the course, he had to carry just under seventy pounds of pack, food and water, plus climbing gear on his 146-pound frame. As a result he had suffered minor knee and lower leg injuries and was forced to semiretire from hiking for nearly nine months following that initial expedition.

The light of a new day was obvious by now. Matthew was in stable condition, and the conversation turned to where to get additional needed medical attention.

"You'll have to take him to the Centro de Salubridad y Asistencia de este distrito (Center of Health and Assistance of this district [Oaxaca])," said the woman. "That is in Pochutla, which is about a half hour drive inland from here."

Manuel then spoke again. "My mother owns a motel/resort not far down the beach, and I know that she would be willing to put you two up in one of her cabanas. Her name is Gloria, and she owns Casa de Gloria. She is part Mexican and part American, as am I. I live in California, but I am here visiting her. I can take you there now, and I am sure that we can get you to Pochutla."

Debra said, "That would be most kind of you. Are you sure your mother won't object?"

"I'm sure," said Manuel.

As it turned out, not only did Gloria offer Matthew and Debra free room and board, she also introduced them to a lady friend named Maria who was visiting and upon hearing about Matthew and Debra's misadventure volunteered to drive them to the medical center in Pochutla.

Are You Sure You Are a Doctor?

DEBRA CLIMBED INTO the backseat, and Matthew gingerly eased himself into the shotgun seat while Maria started up Gloria's Volkswagen Rabbit, which was showing signs of rust as most vehicles near the ocean did. Debra and Maria made small talk while Matthew stared numbly out the windshield barely noticing the rural countryside of Mexico as he was lost in reliving the previous hours of surprise and trauma.

Soon they arrived in the town of Pochutla where Maria easily found the clinic which by American standards didn't look at all like a place where one would receive medical treatment. The stuccoed walls of the one-story square building were badly in need of repair, and one of the three small windows facing the dirt parking area had a large crack running mostly diagonally from top to bottom. Exiting the Rabbit, they entered the centro and found a middle-aged Mexican woman sitting at a small desk wearing an all-white nurse's uniform and a rather tall, handsome Mexican also wearing a traditional white smock with a stethoscope hanging around his neck, the sensor stuck in a breast pocket. Doctors did this for two main reasons: the first being to take some of the weight of the sensor off of their necks, and the second being to keep the sensor from harm's way, as it would tend to dangle and bump into things—including patients—as the doctor would lean forward to attend to them or write a prescription. Matthew knew this because he had observed that practice of protecting the stethoscope by his father who was a doctor practicing family medicine in a rural community in southern Colorado having stopped practicing neurosurgery some years previously due to a hand injury.

Debra and Matthew and Gloria's friend collaborated to inform the doctor and his nurse about the preceding night's events and fill out a few forms before Matthew and Debra were escorted into an examination room. Matthew inspected his surroundings as he always did when going to a place where he had never been before. He noticed how spartan the room was, containing but a single wooden chair, an examination table, a tiny shelf/cupboard combination in one corner of the room with a few boxes of Band-Aids and 2x2s, 4x4s, a pair of surgical scissors, and a box of plastic gloves. There was also a handmade wooden cross hanging from a small nail which had cracked the stucco finish when it had been mounted. The walls looked similar to the exterior building walls in that there were numerous spots where the stucco was missing exposing the underlayment of mud and straw composition. The room looked and felt clean, but not sterile. Matthew eased himself onto the solid table as instructed by the doctor and removed Debra's t-shirt. He had multiple upper body wounds which the doctor wanted to examine first before turning his attention to the head wound.

Although the doctor did speak and understand some English, he welcomed Gloria's friend's interpretation of the preceding night's events as Matthew and Debra recalled how they were initially just victims of robbery, but because they had resisted also become victims of assault. As the doctor examined each wound it became clear that Matthew had been very lucky in that he had been struck with the flat side of the robbers' machetes; each of the five attackers had one such tool or as they had been used in this case, weapon. In all, Matthew had been slapped on his left upper arm and right lower arm, his chest, the calf muscle of his right leg, and most aggressively on the very top of his head. The doctor, as Debra later informed Matthew, directed in

Spanish his nurse-assistant to clean the body wounds while he did a more thorough examination of the open head wound.

"This needs four or five stitches, so I'll need for you to lie down," he said in Spanish which was then translated to Matthew. As he was pretty well exhausted by that time, Matthew gratefully followed the doctor's request. After placing a pillow under Matthew's neck and one under his knees, the doctor began to do some further cleaning around the wound. Matthew then began to scan the new view—the ceiling. Immediately he noticed that there was a good-sized spider web in one of the corners of the ceiling where it met the off-white wall. There was a thumb-sized spider and numerous insects tangled in its web. *Either these people don't look up when they clean around here or they appreciate the spider helping keep the gnat and fly populations under control*, thought Matthew. A faint smile crossed his lips. He wanted to talk about what he was observing but thought better of it, realizing that it might be better not to distract the doctor from focusing on sewing up his head. Later, he would tell Debra about the innocent arachnid he had observed while lying on the examination table.

In less than twenty minutes the doctor sewed up Matthew's head wound, dressed it with a 4x4 and tape, and helped Matthew sit back up and slip on the borrowed t-shirt. He had no other patients, which explained why he was so attentive to Matthew. Gloria's friend, who by then had come into the examination room to see how things were going, and the doctor left the examination room together to settle up the bill as the nurse and Debra helped Matthew off the exam table. He was by now quite exhausted and still light-headed. Debra thanked the nurse and the doctor for their help and understanding while holding on to Matthew's arm. Then she escorted him back to the Rabbit. Debra offered to repay Maria just as soon as she could, but she dismissed Debra's offer saying, "De nada. I am just glad that I could help out in some way."

"No, no. We want to repay you," said Debra.

"It's okay. I sympathize with your situation. Besides I can afford to do this for you. Don't worry about it."

"Are you sure?"

"I'm sure."

Before heading back to Gloria's there was a matter of business which had to be dealt with and that was the filing of a police report. According to Gloria the place to do that was also in Portchutla. Following directions obtained from the doctor's assistant Maria dropped Matthew and Debra off while she ran a personal errand. The process of filing their report became rather tedious because the officer taking Debra and Matthew's report had limited knowledge of the English language. However after a while the policeman and Debra started to communicate with greater understanding of each other and their collaboration produced a one page narrative in Spanish. After asking for and receiving a copy of the report they left the station and after a short while looked up to see Maria returning to pick them up.

On the way back to Casa de Gloria, Matthew faded in and out of sleep, and Debra did her best to stay awake while also making small talk with their new benefactor. When they arrived back at the hacienda, there was a brief discussion with Gloria, who also totally understood the travelers' predicament and offered a cabana (as Manuel had predicted) to Matthew and Debra, adding that they would be welcome to stay as long as needed and that they could pay her later. Debra did most of the talking, thanking Gloria and promising to repay her. Gloria escorted them a very short distance to their temporary home, where they thanked Gloria again. Debra watched Gloria head back up to the main resort and turned to Matthew and exchanged a knowing glance before removing their sandals. They then layed down on a queen-sized futon and promptly fell into a deep sleep, although it was only midday on the fourth day of their adventure. They would sleep through the rest of the afternoon and evening and not stir until early the next morning.

As the new day broke, Debra awoke, and as she was stirring around and checking her backpack, Matthew also awoke. "How are you feeling?" she asked.

"Like I just played a game of football," he replied while rolling himself up to a sitting position.

"I'm feeling hungry," said Debra. It had been well over a day since either one of them had eaten. "How about you, or do you even feel like eating?"

"Yes, a bit. I'm more thirsty than hungry though. But how are we going to pay for anything?"

Matthew had been so out of it when they had arrived at Casa de Gloria that he missed out on most of the conversations that Debra and Gloria had had, including the reassurance that they were welcome to stay and eat for as long as it took to get their situation straightened out.

"Gloria is taking care of us," reassured Debra.

With concerted effort Matthew pushed himself up and with a steadying hand from Debra kicked his feet into his sandals—the only item of personal clothing he had left after the banditos had made off with all the rest of his possessions including his and Debra's visas, their return-flight airline tickets, and traveler's checks. As the adventurers made their way up the short walk to the main structure of Casa de Gloria, the critical problem facing them began to sink in. Not only were they without any money, more importantly their visas, both of which had been conveniently stashed in Matthew's backpack, were gone, which meant that they couldn't get out of Mexico without the proof that they were actually citizens of the United States. It was a sobering realization for Matthew more so than for Debra, who had already begun to worry about their situation.

When they reached the main dining area of Casa de Gloria, which was an open-air structure consisting of large supporting posts throughout the room with handsomely oil-stained ceiling joists and roof rafters supporting a thatched roof, they joined a few other thirty-something-year-olds for a continental breakfast consisting of homemade pastries, whole wheat bread for toasting, bananas, slices of pineapples and mangos, red and green grapes, various boxes of cereals including some Fruit Loops, which seemed odd but apparently in high demand by the younger crowd that frequently stayed at Gloria's. There were also coffee and various teas, but what first caught Matthew's attention were some blueberry filled croissants piled neatly on an attractively hand-painted heavy platter next to the teas and coffee. Likewise, Debra chose a croissant, only hers was filled with strawberry jelly. They served themselves some scrambled eggs, still warm in a stainless-steel steam table pan, added some grapes and a banana to their plates, and looked up to find a table.

There were plenty of tables to choose from, as there were only one young couple and two guys occupying separate tables. They all acknowledged the newcomers with warm smiles, and the young man and woman offered a table next to them. Matthew and Debra accepted their offer, sat down, and began a conversation which quickly led into how Matthew was doing. He said that he was doing okay; however, he soon realized that that was stretching the truth. He took a bite of his blueberry croissant, tried some eggs, then put his fork back down on his plate at the four o'clock position and began instead to sip his chamomile tea. He simply had little appetite and realized that he was very, very tired. For a while he tried to engage in the conversation that was developing, but soon found that he had an overwhelming urge to go back to their cabana and get more rest. The previous day's events had caught up with him, and he subconsciously realized that he could not just "carry on" with his adventure with Debra. He needed rest and he needed it now. He excused himself from the table and went back to the cabana overlooking the ocean, where he promptly fell to sleep. Matthew was listening to his body talk to him. It was a concept that he had begun embracing ever since moving to the community of Breckenridge in 1971. There he met so many young, new age thinkers who were themselves accepting the mantras of "be your own doctor" and "listen to your body." And so, that is what he did. Meanwhile, Debra politely carried on a conversation with the young couple who turned out to be from Australia on their own adventure before also excusing herself to go check on Matthew. After satisfying herself that he was okay, she pulled out a paperback book from her pack and began to read, but before too long found that she too was being overtaken by the lack of sleep. She then laid down next to Matthew and also fell into a long, morning nap as the sound of the ocean's waves continually rolled up and broke apart on the beach below.

Near midday Debra awoke feeling rested but restless. Matthew, on the other hand, continued to sleep, still in the same position in which Debra had found him several hours before. She decided to take a walk and explore the grounds of Casa de Gloria. She put on some sunscreen, grabbed her sun hat, and headed down a well-traveled path toward the beach below. She hadn't gone too far before she stopped to marvel at the scene before her. The blue-green waves continued to roll in onto the off-white sand, churning up a foamy grey mix of water and sand before spreading out so delicately across the endless beach, while directly below her the same waves came crashing into the jagged lava rocks tossing the waves high and wide only to come pounding down causing the crashing sound written so often about in poems and prose. Debra looked back toward the gentler waves further down the beach and thought how wonderful it would feel to go swimming. *Perhaps I'll wait until Matthew feels better to do that*, she thought.

Nine Lost Days at Casa de Gloria

IT WAS NOW DAY FIVE of Matthew and Debra's adventure, and things were not going as they had loosely planned. And yet they were. They were hanging out on a beautiful beach in Mexico where the average daytime temperature was 82 degrees, and they were eating well on very little money—in fact, none. The banditos had taken Matthew's backpack with all of Matthew's possessions except for his sandals, tent, sleeping bag, and sleeping pad. Gone were all his clothes, a Kodak Instamatic camera, and several extra rolls of film on which he and Debra had planned to record their trip. He had also lost his visa, his passport, $115.00 in cash, over 3,700 pesos, and eight twenty-dollar traveler's checks, not to mention their return-flight airline tickets. Debra had shared this news with Matthew after he had received his initial medical attention and that her small yellow daypack with all of her money, visa, and birth certificate had also been stolen by the robbers. The good news was that the universe was taking care of them. They had the basics for survival plus more. Thanks to the goodness of Gloria and her staff, they had the bare necessities for life: water, food, and shelter. And what a fine shelter it was—a cabana perched on a knoll overlooking the Pacific Ocean with its continuous wave action beckoning one to either sleep restfully immersed in its lullaby or to plunge into an oncoming single roll of water with the anticipation of emerging from its smooth backside to be buoyed by the saltwater where one's cares would float away.

Matthew's condition chose the first option for him, whereas the tantalizing ocean lured Debra to the second option. So, the next day while Matthew was sleeping once again, Debra grabbed her towel and headed to the beach where there appeared to be no one else. She had heard through her conversations with locals and a couple from France that swimwear was optional on the beaches of Zipolite; so she looked up and down the beach, and seeing no one, she kicked off her sandals, slipped out of her shorts, underwear, and short-sleeved top and sprinted bare naked to the welcoming water. As soon as the first big wave nearly reached her, she dove into its falling roll of warm Pacific water as she was embarrassed by her nakedness and wanted to be covered up by the blue-green water as quickly as possible. How wonderful the moment felt as she ducked under another wave that seemed warmer than the first and holding her breath swam underwater for several strokes feeling so alive and invigorated by her secret skinny-dip in the vast ocean of the Pacific.

Upon surfacing, Debra turned to look back at the beach and, noticing how uplifting the saltwater was, she brought her hand up to shield her eyes from the brilliant sun and quickly spotted the roof of the cabana in which Matthew lay convalescing. A twinge of sadness passed through her mind as she wished he were sharing the luxuriating moment with her.

Just then another wave rolled up and down past her, not breaking, just picking her up and lowering her gently back down, but as she noticed with a bit of concern, she was floating away from the beach.

Better not get too far from the shoreline, she thought wisely as she knew how powerful waves could be despite their alluring beauty. Treading easily in the saltwater, she turned her head to look for the next wave thinking she would bodysurf it back inland toward the beach. As another smooth roll of water caught and lifted her, she extended her naked body and began to swim mostly on top of the buoyant saltwater, but after a half-dozen arm strokes and leg kicks, she realized that she was basically no closer to the shore. With that realization suddenly filling her mind, she began to swim harder. As she did so another wave swept in from behind her, picked her up, and lowered her quickly back down on the backside of the wave which, to her horror, was pulling her further from the beach.

The name of the beach—Playa de Zipolite—was an innocent enough name that meant "place of continuous bumps or hills" until one found out what its reputation meant—"beach of the dead!" There had been numerous deaths recorded at Playa de Zipolite due to drowning as unsuspecting swimmers were caught by the powerful undertow of the waves. Even the strongest of swimmers could be pulled out to sea and eventually drowned by the undertow. Debra was a good swimmer and a strong woman, but no match for those waves.

Debra realized then that she had no other choice but to stroke with her arms and kick with her legs with all her might toward the beach. Unfortunately, she was aware that, slowly but surely, she was indeed being swept seaward while thinking, perhaps praying, that this wasn't happening. It wasn't long before she became exhausted and was having trouble getting enough air. So she stopped swimming and rolled onto her back in order to keep her mouth and nose out of the water more easily and perhaps catch her breath.

Suddenly she realized someone was next to her and had grabbed her between the legs and started dragging her towards the beach with powerful leg kicks and right-arm swim strokes. She made a quick decision to relax as much as she could and trust this strong swimmer to pull her to the beach. And as she did so, she realized that this exceptional swimmer was a brown-skinned man, probably a local, who most likely had spotted her swimming into danger before she realized it herself. Debra's mind raced with thoughts of now-subsiding panic, embarrassment as she remembered that she was naked in the ocean with a stranger who just then released his grip from her crotch, and how she was going to tell Matthew about what had just happened. Regaining some composure, she rolled over into the next wave and, facing her rescuer while treading the now calmer waters nearer the beach, blurted out, "Thank you, gracias," and quickly turned back toward the beach. Then she began to swim furiously to the beach where she stood up, looked frantically for and spotted her clothes, and began to run to them hoping that no one was watching her running naked across the beach. But, of course, someone was watching. Her rescuer, still bobbing up and down with each new wave, was watching her. He smiled and then dove under the next wave.

Debra quickly reached for her clothing and, not bothering to towel off, dressed and scampered back to the cabana and a shower. As she showered off the saltwater, she decided that she would wait to tell Matthew what had just happened. She was fully aware that she had put herself in harm's way twice now in less than a week. Her mind was still racing with images of the past half hour. Debra closed her eyes, took a deep breath, and, as she exhaled, began to feel the warm shower water wash away her worries.

It was a few days later when Matthew finally had the strength to get up and move about. Feeling more energized he and Debra made a new plan. They figured that in order to get back to the United States they would have to get some documentation to prove their citizenship and that the place to secure such papers was the US embassy in Mexico City. However, to get there and be able to have some money to buy meals and pay for at least one night's lodging, they would need some cash. So, Matthew, who was by now feeling more clearheaded, told Debra that he was confident that if he called his boss back in Breckenridge, Colorado, he could convince him to wire some money.

"I'll call Bruce [that was his boss's first name] collect when we find out where a telegraph office is," said Matthew.

Debra agreed that that would be their best strategy. When they asked as to the location of the nearest pay phone and telegraph office, they found out that they would have to return to Pochutla. At that moment they realized just how far they had traveled off the beaten path of civilization. The closest pay phone was a good half-hour's drive inland.

And so, they went to their open-air room, got their sun hats—Matthew's had not been in his pack when it was stolen—smeared on some sunscreen, and began to hitchhike to Pochutla. After walking for a while along a dusty road that did offer some shade from the summer sun, a well-tanned Caucasian driving a rather beat up Volkswagen bus—a 1970 or 1971 model, Matthew guessed—slowed and pulled up beside them. Debra and Matthew had been standing just off the narrow road flashing the universal hitchhiker's request for a ride, although Matthew's hand lay palm open as opposed to the traditional rolled up fingers with the thumb up being used by Debra. He had been using this adaptation ever since the year 1976 while hitching rides to the Pacific Northwest. He had been hitching one summer's day and started to notice how tired his right hand was getting from holding the four-finger fist position for hours. So, as he stared almost mindlessly at his fingers at the end of his outstretched arm, he allowed his fingers to unfold, and it felt so relaxing that he kept it that way as the next vehicle approached. To his amazement and relief, a car stopped and gave him a ride. He surmised that the open hand was a friendlier gesture appearing like an offered handshake perhaps and therefore more appealing to drivers checking him out as they approached.

The bus driver offered up a toothy smile through the open window on the passenger side of his van and said, "A donde van?"

"Pochutla," Debra said quickly as she was more well versed in conversational Spanish than Matthew.

"Entran" said the driver. Matthew deftly opened the sliding back door while Debra got in the front seat and, with a combination of Spanish and English, she was able to get a rough idea as to where the oficina de telegrafo was located and that the driver would be able to let them off near there.

Soon they reached the outskirts of Pochutla where they were dropped off and with a vague idea as to where to find the telegraph building set off walking. The unpaved streets were lined with whitewashed adobe buildings whose walls were mostly faded, cracked, and peeling, especially on the alley walls. It wasn't long before they realized how dehydrated they had become, and their focus switched from searching for the telegraph office and noticing the simplicity of the town to finding something to drink. Perhaps by divine intervention just a short time later Matthew spotted what appeared to be a coin laying in the street. Reaching down, he discovered that there were actually two coins—a couple of pesos—which he quickly picked up. As he blew some dust off the coins, he said, "Looky here, Debra. We're rich!"

She was elated, but not surprised that Matthew had found the money, for he had always had a knack for doing that. Within minutes the thirsty couple found an open market stand that was selling local fruits and vegetables, and there in the middle of the bananas and oranges sat a large, clear-glass jug of what appeared to be orange juice.

"Hola. Es este jugo de naranja?" said Debra to the vendor while Matthew eyed the jug which he noticed had condensation because it was sitting in a shallow pottery platter with a small amount of ice.

"Si, señora."

"Cuánto cuesta?" inquired Debra.

"Dos pesos," replied the vendor. "Quieres dos vasos?"

"Uno," said Matthew, understanding the question while holding up the pointer finger of his right hand and offering his two pesos with his left. The vendor filled a glass with a long-handled wooden ladle and handed it to Matthew. Taking the glass and thanking the vendor, Matthew immediately sat down with Debra at one of the two sets of small tables and chairs sitting nearby in the shade of a two-story stucco building. They sipped and savored the chilled glass of orange juice, holding each sip for extra enjoyment before swallowing, and each time they swallowed it was followed by a totally satisfying "Yummmmm." It was the best tasting orange juice ever!

Having quenched their thirst and being slightly energized, the couple started walking again in search of the telegraph office which, if Debra had understood the driver correctly, would be found at the intersection two blocks ahead. And sure enough, they found it in a one-story building set back slightly from the street. As it turned out, the adjacent building had several bank teller-like windows where one could place phone calls with the assistance of a telephone operator. To Matthew and Debra's pleasant surprise, both the telegraph office and the phone windows were open for business.

There was a line of people—seven to be exact—waiting patiently to make phone calls. At that moment there were two phone conversations going on right out in public as the callers were given no privacy. A handset was passed through the window. The operator listened from the inside, and everyone in line had the opportunity to eavesdrop from the outside.

"I hope Bruce is in his office this morning," said Matthew.

"Do you remember the BOEC's number?" asked Debra. "If not, I do," she replied with confidence, as she had called Matthew at work many times.

"I do remember it. I hope he'll accept my collect call," Matthew said. "I sure as heck don't want to have to call my parents and ask them for money and have to explain everything to them, especially not out here in public, although I'll bet there aren't any English language speakers in line."

Matthew looked around to see if anyone appeared to be paying attention to what he had just said. No one appeared interested. However, Matthew would soon lose that hypothetical bet, and it would be a good thing.

"I do hope, though, that the phone operator speaks English."

"Next," said a voice from behind one of the two arched window openings. Each window had a protruding shelf. They moved forward, and Matthew, upon seeing a Mexican woman who offered up a pleasant smile, said, "Buenos días."

"Buenos días, señor. How can I help you?" Relieved that she spoke English, Matthew stated his business: "I would like to place a call to the United States."

"All right, sir. And what is the name and number of the place that you want to call?"

"It is called the Breckenridge Outdoor Education Center for the Handicapped, and the number is 970-453-6422." Matthew apologized that it was such a long name.

"Si, that is a very long name. Would you repeat it, please?"

Matthew repeated the name of his place of work and added his own name for further clarification.

"Un momento, por favor," said the operator. "Will you be paying with cash or traveler's checks?"

"Neither one. I need to make this a collect call," said Matthew.

Holding her hand over the speaker end of the standard-colored black handset, the operator said, "I am sorry, sir, but we do not allow collect calls here. You must pay first."

"But I have no money, and I don't have a credit card. Can't you please let me call my boss in the United States? I know he will accept the charge."

"I'm sorry, sir, but like I said, we do not allow collect calls here. You must pay first to place a call."

Matthew turned to Debra with a shocked look and was met with her own look of disbelieve, whereupon she began to cry.

"I can't believe this is happening to us," she sobbed. Debra then turned to the telephone operator and explained using her best Spanish, "We can't pay for a phone call because we have no money because we were robbed on your beaches and . . . ." The end of her sentence became a short string of inarticulate sounds as her sobbing increased.

Just then they heard someone next to them say, "I'll pay for the call." The words came from a man standing in front of the other window. Debra and Matthew turned simultaneously to see a handsome, thirty-something-year-old Mexican dressed in a smart-looking business suit.

"Really?" responded Debra, suddenly regaining her composure and wiping away her tears. "That would be so kind of you. Thank you, thank you."

"Si, si, gracias, señor," said Matthew.

The Mexican gentleman stepped over to the window, spoke briefly in his native tongue to the operator, and asked the stranded couple where they needed to call. Matthew quickly replied, "The number is 970-453-6422. Ask for Mr. Bruce Weber. My name is Matthew Sheldon." The operator placed the call as the gentleman stranger gave her some money. The operator handed the phone to Matthew, and he listened intently to the distant ringing.

"Hello," said a voice. "This is the Breckenridge Outdoor Education Center for the Handicapped. This is Bruce speaking. How can I help you?"

Just the words he needed to hear, thought Matthew. After exchanging, "Hi, how are you?" Matthew explained his and Debra's situation to his boss before asking him if he would take care of their needs including paying Gloria for their lodging and meals, but the gentleman benefactor politely interrupted and strongly cautioned against having large sums of money wired to Pochutla. Apparently, it was widely known by the locals that wired money frequently disappeared from the telegraph offices next door. The telephone operator nodded in agreement. "Si, señor, este es verdad."

Matthew and Debra quickly calculated that they could make do with $150, if upon receiving that money, they were to leave Mexico in the next day or two. Matthew explained to Bruce the caution about sending too much money given to him as Bruce told Matthew he trusted him for whatever amount he wanted. Bruce said no problem to the $150 as the details of the transaction were discussed and that he would get on it right away. Matthew covered the speaker end of the handset, and asked Debra if she had anything else to add.

"Just tell him thank you so much for being there and for helping us."

Matthew did so, said goodbye, and with reluctance handed the phone back to the operator through the tiny arched window frame. He felt uneasy letting go of their only real connection to the safety and security of their home back in the States.

Matthew and Debra moved out of line and turned their attention back to the gentleman in the other line who was by that time busy with his own phone. Realizing that Matthew had completed his phone call, he said, "Un momento, por favor" to whomever he was talking to, covered the speaker end of the handset, and said, in English, "I'm glad I could help. Buena suerte."

"THANK YOU," said Matthew and Debra more or less in unison.

There was nothing else they could do. The process of wiring money was mostly a mystery. Adding to the mystery was the fact that the process took so long. The two Americans from Colorado were advised that they might as well take in the sights and sounds of Mexico, as it would take weeks, maybe months, before they would possibly receive wired money from the US. With that sobering thought in mind Debra and Matthew headed back to Zipolite.

By the time they were able to get back to Casa de Gloria, it was midafternoon and because Gloria's place, like many hotels with attached restaurant facilities, only served a breakfast and a dinner, there was only water and a bowl of fruits—some mangos, some green grapes, and one ripe banana left over from the morning meal—to be found upon entering the resturant. Being almost like beggars, they took some of the fruit including the one slightly browning banana and devoured it while washing it down with lots of fresh, but by now air-temperature water. But none of that mattered. It all tasted heavenly.

They returned to their cabana overlooking the tumbling waves that kept so many secrets and laid down to review the day's events. Feeling weary from the day's emotional ups and downs plus the lack of nutrition, they soon fell asleep. By the time they would awake, it was the beginning of the dinner hour—six o'clock—and that was just fine with them, for they were quite hungry. After splashing some water on their faces, toweling off, and Debra running her comb through her long red hair, they made their way up the walkway to the dining area of Casa de Gloria. They proceeded to politely devour some homemade chicken enchiladas with mixed salad greens, tomatoes, and two kinds of shredded cheese. They followed that with a dessert: hot sopapillas to which they added butter and honey. As they sat there in the open-air dining area and savored their first satisfying meal in a week, their thoughts and conversation ran in a circle.

"Well, what shall we do now?" said Matthew.

"Let's take a walk along the beach."

"Okay. And let's make it a long, slow one because it won't be dark for hours, and we have plenty of time to waste."

"That's for sure. And tomorrow, what do you want to do?"

"Don't know. Guess we'll think of something. Perhaps we could go for a walk on the beach," said Matthew wryly.

"Ha-ha," laughed Debra.

The ensuing days and nights were filled with many walks, naps, reading, and idle talk as the penniless tourists from Colorado tried not to think about how stranded they were and were constantly reminding each other that they were in relative paradise and that they should try and make the best of the situation. After all, they weren't destitute. They did have food, water, and shelter. But, as they talked, they both revealed to one another that their subconscious minds wouldn't let go of the fact that they were in a foreign country with no proof of who they were or citizenship and they had no money. It was a very worrisome thought.

The part of the daily routine that came the easiest for Matthew was the napping, because he was not consuming enough calories because he still didn't have much of an appetite. He was still slowly but surely recovering from the beating he took on the beach. As they finished breakfast one morning, Debra said that she had met a couple of ladies staying at Casa de Gloria who found out about a spot next to a stream nearby where they could do some laundry and bathe and that the three of them were planning to go there that day. So, Matthew wished her a good time and headed back to their room for some reading and more rest.

A few hours later Matthew was up again and made his way to the dining area which also served as a living room where guests could gather most any time of the day. As he entered the space, he smiled as he spotted Debra who was just leaving a small group consisting of Gloria and some other women, presumably the ones she had gone to the stream with for bathing and washing clothes. Matthew could sense that something was up and that Gloria was upset because she did not acknowledge him, something she had done consistently during their time there.

"What's up?" asked Matthew as Debra came over to him.

"We just told Gloria that we were harassed by federales on our way back from the stream, and she is furious. She said they have no right to disturb guests and tourists, and she went on to explain how it hurts her business when people like us—her guests—are bothered by soldiers, especially when there is no reason for them to be doing so," explained Debra.

"What did the federales do?" inquired Matthew as he moved to the table that held a pottery jug of water and some ceramic cups.

"Oh, they stopped us and demanded to check our bags which contained our wet undergarments. It was strange and embarrassing."

"I see your point," responded Matthew. "And I can see why this incident with the federales could really hurt her business. I bet Gloria will be having an animated conversation with some local base commander very soon. Anyway, I see you still have wet clothes ready to hang up. Thank goodness those soldiers didn't confiscate them," said Matthew. He was still wearing one of the only two pairs of shorts that Debra had brought on their trip. "So, did you really clean your clothes by beating them on some rocks?"

"Yes, just like they did it in the old days and no doubt like it is done in many parts of the world today, including Mexico. It worked for me."

Early the next morning word came that their money had arrived at the telegraph office. The robbery victims were completely surprised that it had arrived so fast after being told by a couple of sources that they would not get any response for weeks, more likely months!

Since it was only mid-morning, they asked around the dining room and scored a ride to Puerto Angel. From there they thumbed a ride to the telegraph office in Pochutla. Still without any form of identification, Matthew and Debra were able to give the telegraph office personnel enough details about who was sending the money and from where the money was being sent plus enough details about the pending transaction that eventually they were handed about 2,900 pesos, which was roughly equivalent to 150 US dollars.

At that point they had hope that they were going to be able to make it back home. So back they went to highway where, once again, they hitchhiked to Puerto Angel and Playa de Zipolite making plans and talking excitedly about their return to the United States. But first, they needed some identification. During the preceding weeks they had found out that once they had some traveling money, the next thing they would have to do would be to see the American consul in Oaxaca. They decided to catch the bus in the morning.

Oaxaca, Oaxaca

TRAVELING TO OAXACA was to be the first leg of their journey back home, but because they had so little to pack up and that they had accomplished their packing in less than half an hour, they decided to take one last walk on the beaches of Zipolite. Buoyed by the day's events, the couple's walk became brand new, despite the fact that they had been there many times in the preceding days. The sand under their feet seemed warmer and more welcoming than before. The ocean breeze was intoxicating as they wandered hand-in-hand towards the lava rock formations that separated the sandy beaches facing the Pacific and the setting of the sun. And what a setting sun it was that evening, as the expansive western sky began to mellow from the brilliant blue of the day into yellow, then bright reds painting the underside of some distant puffy clouds whose meteorological names neither one of them could remember.

As they neared the ocean-smoothed rocks, they were surprised by another couple who waved and invited Matthew and Debra to come over to their campfire. As they accepted the invitation and neared the new couple, they began to see that it was more than just a campfire by the ocean; rather it was a full camp site with pots and pans and backpacks and an out-stretched tarp under which there was a second tarp with camp pads and one blue and another green-blue sleeping bag laid out neatly. In many of the hollowed-out pockets of the rocks the couple had set various camp items like cups and silverware along with a small pair of binoculars and some paperback books whose titles they could not see. It turned out that they were an English couple on an extended vacation and were living there by the sea and had been there for a month! They offered Debra and Matthew some wine, and after an hour or so of sipping their drinks and exchanging stories—the couple had already heard of Matthew and Debra's ordeal by word of mouth and perhaps took pity on them, or perhaps just because they were such outgoing people to begin with—they invited the travelers from Colorado to stay for dinner. Debra accepted the offer for the two of them, and Matthew and Debra plopped down somewhat near the campfire and were soon sinking into the warm sand as the wine and the evening and the warmth of the campfire were topped off with some freshly caught ocean fish so delicious that Matthew just could not stop eating the saltwater catch.

But the following morning, he wished he could have exercised more restraint at the previous night's dinner by the sea, because now he was sick to his stomach. Whether it was because he had eaten too much freshly caught sea food, or that perhaps the fish was not fully cooked over the open fire, or even perhaps his stomach just was not accustomed to being filled, the indisputable fact was that now he was sick as a dog.

But that was not going to stop him from beginning their journey back home. Pushing through the nausea, he and Debra, who felt fine, put their few remaining items in Debra's backpack and made their way up to the dining area looking for Gloria to thank her for all that she had done and to assure her that just as soon as they got back home they would be sending her money to cover their nearly three weeks of lodging and food which she had graciously fronted them. Gloria seemed to be relieved that they were moving on and would stop being a drain on her restaurant's bottom line, but nevertheless she gave each of them a hug and wished them safe passage home.

Leaving Gloria's Pacific Ocean paradise was bittersweet, and after taking one last walk on the beach, they started walking back to Puerto Angel where they would catch the bus that would take them to Oaxaca some five hours away. They did have a phone number and a name—a

Ms. Barbara French, an American consul, whom they would contact once they were in Oaxaca.

The forty-five-minute walk helped a bit, but the nausea persisted as the now noticeably skinnier Matthew and the tanner Debra boarded the bus, paid the driver, and found seats on the shotgun side of the bus with Matthew opting to sit next to the window, which he immediately cracked open just enough to give himself fresh air, but not too wide open to be an inconvenience to those who sat in the seats behind him. Life was uncomplicated in that part of the world, and at the moment that suited Matthew just fine. He just wanted to sit down and close his eyes and hoped that sooner than later he would feel better.

The bus left Puerto Angel just after 10 AM and soon was snaking its way through the Sierra Madre de Oaxaca forests. Debra sat silently next to Matthew, for she was sympathetic to his condition and knew that he did not want to talk let alone look at the lush forest scenery. What a scene he was missing, she thought, as she had not ever seen this tapestry of pine trees and oak trees growing side by side. Her thoughts were mixed as she contemplated the past weeks of warmth and sandy beaches and the ever-changing beauty of the ocean, all spent hoping for this day in which they would be on their way home. Matthew was curled up against the side of the bus, slightly under the window frame, taking long deep breaths in through his nose followed by exhalations through pursed lips which gave him moments of relief despite the back and forth sway of the bus as it followed the continuous curves of the road.

A couple of hours would pass before Matthew, in a semiconscious state, realized that the bus was starting to slow down. He lifted his head, blinking open his eyes against the flickering sunlight as it filtered its way through the evergreens that lined the road. Small buildings and homes and a store front began to reveal themselves. Before the bus came to a complete stop, the next thing that he noticed was about a half-dozen children who were running up to the bus carrying small trays which were supported by straps drapped around their necks. They came right up to the bus and began chattering the familiar English words, "Coca Cola, 7-Up, Chiclets," and in Spanish, "rolles dulces, plátanos," which upon observation of their wares must have meant sweet rolls and bananas, respectively. It was a very good way to learn the language—putting an object with a spoken word—Matthew thought. He was thankful for the moment of respite from the nausea that still plagued him. Suddenly he had an inspiration. He stood up and squeezed the metal window latches to lower the top half of the bus window. Then he put his hand and face partially out through the opening, waved at the closest small boy, and said, "Coca Cola, por favor." Turning back to Debra, he asked her how to say "how much" in Spanish.

"Cuánto cuesta," she answered.

Turning back to the young boy, he said, "Cuánto cuesta?"

The young boy answered, "Seventy-five centavos!"

Again turning to Debra, Matthew asked, "Do you want anything?"

"Yes, get me a banana. The word is 'plátano.'"

To the vendor Matthew asked in his imperfect Spanish, "Cuánto cuesta por una plátano?"

"Seventy-five centavos," was the answer from the young vendor not minding Matthew's imperfect use of Spanish. Apparently everything was seventy-five centavos. *Smart business practice*, thought Matthew.

"Una Coca Cola y un plátano?" asked the young boy.

Matthew proudly responded, "Si," having fully understood what the boy had said in Spanish.

The boy opened a glass bottle of Coca Cola and handed it and a just-ripe banana to Matthew. Matthew gave him forty pesos, as Debra reminded him to add a tip. "Gracias," said Matthew.

"Gracias, señor."

It was the 1980s, and few people paid attention to how much sugar was in a bottle of soda nor to the side effects of consuming so much sugar, but one thing Matthew knew was that sodas had carbonation, and as he took a long, slow swig of the Coke he could feel the bubbles settling in his upset stomach. Soon he got the desired results—a burp. Not your average polite puff of air, but a tremendous belch that surprised even Matthew in its strength and volume. BURRRRRRRP!!!! The relief from the nausea that had been with him ever since rising that morning was instantaneous, and it felt wonderful. So, again he drank some Coke and again he burped and again he felt more relief. And as he consumed the rest of the bottle, the tremendous feeling of relief swept throughout his whole body.

"Better?" asked Debra, knowing full well that he was, judging by the huge smile that came to Matthew's face, as well as the change of facial color from pale to pink once again.

"Oh yeah!" By now the bus driver, who had left the bus, presumably for a bathroom break, returned. He did a quick head count, sat down, and turned the ignition over. Sweet Jesus, that was the best Coke he had ever drunk, thought Matthew.

Less than three hours later, the bus pulled into the city of Oaxaca where everyone including Matthew and Debra exited. Calling the number they had obtained before leaving Zipolite, they were able to speak with the American consul, who although at first was hesitant to meet them until the next day changed her mind after hearing how dire their situation was and graciously invited them to her home. Fortune was still with them that day, as it turned out to be only a twenty-minute walk to the consulate. When they arrived, they pushed a button beneath a small speaker mounted on the stuccoed pillar that supported a cast-iron gate that barred them from entering the premises. Shortly, a voice asked, "Yes?"

"Hello," said Debra. "I am the American tourist that spoke with you about half an hour ago."

"Ah, yes. I'll be there in a moment."

As promised, a rather tall and slim woman, probably in her fifties, walked through the heavy ground level door of what in the States would have been referred to as a two-story townhome. As she neared the cast-iron gate, the lock clicked as she pointed a handheld remote that caused a hidden drive to slowly swing the heavy gate open.

"Come in, welcome. My name is Barbara, Ms. Barbara French," said their host, turning her attention back to the weary travelers. Consuls are trained to listen and observe, and Ms. French noticed right off the pitiful condition Matthew was in after weeks of hardly eating, combined with the fact that he was a thin man to begin with, weighing just 140 pounds when he left the United States.

"My name is Matthew Sheldon; and this, as you already know, is Debra, Debra Beard. We are most grateful to meet you."

"You do appear to need some help. Let us start off with a traditional Mexican supper prepared by a traditional American cook who loves Mexican food. Do you like smothered burritos?"

"Oh yes," said Debra and Matthew as they turned and looked at each other with widening smiles, knowing that they were free to relax for a while.

Ms. French ushered them into her home through a large wooden door smartly decorated on either side by two elaborately crafted cast-iron lamps which were mounted on the brownish stuccoed wall of the townhome. Ms. French once again activated the remote to close the iron barrier. "We Americans are welcome here in Mexico by much of the population, but not by all, but I think you already know that."

The gate clicked shut, and their host shut and locked the apartment door behind them as they ascended some stairs that led to the living area of her home. Because there was still daylight left, the abundantly windowed second floor was most welcoming, with colorful tapestries and bunches of dried red chili peppers hanging by kitchen cupboards mounted craftily above a stainless-steel sink and a brilliantly colored red, blue, turquoise, and yellow tiled countertop.

"Please have a seat. Can I offer you something to drink? I have water, juice, or wine."

"Wine," said Debra.

"The same for me," said Matthew.

"I was hoping that would be your choice," said Ms. French. "I was going to have some myself about the time you called, but I decided to wait until you got here. It's always better when you get the chance to have wine with others. Red or white?"

"Red," responded Debra.

"Make mine red also," said Matthew.

"I'm going to start those burritos I promised you," said Ms. French while filling three long-stemmed wine glasses with a semi-dry red which she confessed was her favorite. "Why don't you tell me more of your story, and we'll figure out how we're going to get you two back home safely."

Their story lasted through all of the preparation time and most of the way through dinner. All the while the consul was judging the validity of the couple's account of the previous week's events. She told them that, unfortunately, she could not do anything for them other than to direct them to the US embassy in Mexico City and give them a lift to the bus depot in the morning. She did confirm that what Matthew and Debra had been told about the telegraph offices in Mexico was true—they were not to be trusted with large sums of money—and that they were, indeed, fortunate that they did receive the small amount of money that had been wired.

The day had slipped into evening and the wine, the delicious meal, and a summer night's breeze all swept over the couple as they helped clear the table and offered to help with the dishes. But their host declined their offer and instead led them to a spare bedroom, pointed out the spare bathroom, and wished them a good night's rest. The weary couple got ready for bed, and sharing Debra's tooth brush brushed their teeth, and crawled into the waiting double bed where they cuddled before falling into an intoxicating sleep.

Assault on the American Embassy

THE FOLLOWING MORNING, they were, as promised, dropped off at the bus depot and soon were on their way to the capital, Mexico City, a five-and-a-half-hour ride through the central part of Mexico which, geographically, was mostly a volcanic plateau. Happy to be heading north, actually northeast, the two Americans gazed out of the bus windows at some distant unknown mountains and stared blankly as they passed by town after town, some actually resembling the "Old Mexico" they had seen in history books. By early afternoon the bus ride was over, and they made yet another short walk, this time to the American Embassy in Ciudad de Mexico. The events of the day were going as expected, but that was about to change.

Walking up to the embassy, the first thing Matthew noticed was the wrought iron fence probably seven or eight feet tall with spiked tops surrounding a compound easily a half a block in size. Moving down the sidewalk, they spotted a short line of citizens in line at what was apparently the main entrance. Matthew and Debra slowed their pace in order to watch and listen as they moved past the entrance to take their place at the end of a line that consisted of six people. As Matthew passed the gated entrance, he noticed a Mexican guard wearing a United States military uniform. Catching some of the conversation between the guard and one of the visitors, he realized they were conversing in part Spanish and part English. As he and Debra stood in line, they overheard more English coming from the guard as he interacted with the next person in line. *This is a good sign*, thought Matthew. With no passports or papers to prove that they were US citizens, at least he and Debra would be able to perhaps talk their way into the embassy. The line moved along quickly and soon it was Debra and Matthew who were next in line.

"Siguiente," said the guard while motioning for the couple to step forward.

"We are American citizens and need to talk to the American consul, por favor," said Matthew, thinking that if he threw in some Spanish he could get on the good side of the uniformed Mexican. "We have been robbed of our passports and need help returning to the United States."

"Yo no hablo inglés," said the guard.

Taken by complete surprise by the response of the guard, Matthew challenged back, "Excuse me? What do you mean you don't speak English? Of course, you do. I just heard you speaking in English with that man you just let in!"

Looking Matthew straight in the eye, the guard once again said, "Yo no hablo inglés."

This time when Matthew spoke, he was visibly annoyed, and he raised his voice and said in a stern manner, "Listen, we need to get inside this embassy to speak to someone! We are broke. We are stuck here in Mexico with no papers. We want to return to the United States."

"Yo no hablo inglés," repeated the guard, now also raising his voice. With the wave of his arm, he motioned for the undocumented Americans to move away from the gate. He then motioned for the next person in line to step forward while ordering "Siguiente!"

Debra took Matthew by the arm and firmly pulled him away from the entrance and the defiant guard. "Come on. We'll think of something else." She meant well, but neither of them had any idea what that "something else" might be.

As they moved down the sidewalk that paralleled the fence of the embassy, Matthew kept turning back to glare at the guard. Suddenly he whispered, "Debra, we have to get inside to see the consul. That's the only way that we are going to make it out of this country."

With little thought as to the consequences and yielding to his emotions that were getting the best of him, Matthew then declared to Debra, "I'm going to climb over the fence." And so, dropping his small bag of possessions and grabbing ahold of two of the iron bars he started to scale the fence.

"Matthew, what the hell are you doing? You're going to get shot!" exclaimed Debra in a somewhat hushed but frantic voice.

"I'm going to try and get some attention."

And attention he got. First from the guard on duty who starting yelling something in Spanish while beginning to unholster his sidearm, but also the attention of a passerby who fortunately recognized what was happening.

"There is another way, a safer way to get into the embassy, my friend," said the man. "I think I can help you get inside to see someone, because I work here."

As Matthew backed down off the fence to face the man who had offered to help, he was not aware that the guard had removed his hand from his sidearm, but Debra had been alternately watching the guard and Matthew and was relieved that Matthew was no longer in danger. Debra then turned her full attention to the embassy worker.

"Thank you. Oh, thank you so much. We were robbed of all of our money and our visas, and we need to see the American consul to see if they can help us get back into the United States," she blurted out.

"I understand. Come with me." The man knew what he was talking about, as he led them back to the embassy gate and spoke in Spanish with the guard, who after a minute aside and waved the three of them inside.

Debra kept her eyes focused on the walkway, but Matthew and the guard exchanged contemptuous looks as the backpackers passed by the guard station, entered the compound, and went inside the US embassy. They then headed up a fine old wooden staircase that creaked with every step. They were introduced to a consul named James Davis. Mr. Davis would be the man to produce the necessary documents: a to-whom-it-may-concern document and a port-of-entry document both of whose purposes where to take the place of the couple's stolen visas and convince any authorities, like an officer in charge at the US Port of Entry, that Matthew and Debra were truly citizens of the United States of America.

After some preliminary small talk, Mr. Davis asked Debra and Matthew to tell him their story mainly to convince himself that they were telling a credible story. They explained what had happened in the early morning hours of the fifth of May and presented a copy of a sworn statement created by an officer in the Judicial District of Oaxaca on the seventh of May. After perhaps forty-five minutes of listening and questions, Mr. Davis opened a desk drawer and pulled out several official United States embassy forms, inserting one of them into a well-used Smith Corona desktop typewriter, and filled in the necessary information explaining who they were, where they lived, and how they came to be in Mexico. Then he typed in a brief summary of what Matthew and Debra had told him followed by two statements: (1) that "by virtue of birth" he was a citizen of the United States, and (2) that he had never committed any act which would result in the loss of his citizenship. It was a one-page, triple-spaced document that Matthew signed. He then created the same documents for Debra which she signed. He then made a copy of each document so that Matthew and Debra each had copies. That was it. Mr. Davis, the American consul at the United States Embassy in Mexico, had created the "get-out-of-jail" cards, so to speak, for Debra and Matthew. In addition to preparing the necessary papers, the consul told them that he would provide them with airline tickets from Mexico City to Ciudad Juarez, but that they would not be available until the next morning. Knowing what a difficult time they had getting into the embassy that day, Mr. Davis reassured them that he would make the necessary arrangements for them to be given safe passage into the embassy compound in the morning.

Then there was the matter of money. They had just about spent all of the money that they had received from the United States sent by Matthew's boss. So, once again, Mr. Davis pulled out yet another form and proposed that if they were willing to sign an IOU to the American Embassy, he was authorized to lend them a small amount of money, in this case 500 pesos, about $125 US. Both of them signed the IOU, and Debra received the $125 which Mr. Davis had taken from a small cash box he had pulled from the same drawer from which he had taken out the IOU.

"That should get you through the rest of the day and tomorrow morning until you board a flight from the Mexico City airport to Ciudad Juarez where you will have to depart the plane and cross the Mexico–US border by car or walking, as it is not possible to fly directly in and out of this country," informed Mr. Davis. "For your information, we frequently have tourists and visitors asking us for help because of lost IDs or passports as well as running out of money, but only rarely do we have folks like you who lose everything to a robbery, especially a crime on the beach. So, we are prepared to help you out."

"Thank you so much for helping us and believing in us enough to lend us money," said Matthew.

"You are most welcome. This is one of our main functions as an embassy, to help visitors in trouble in a foreign country in time of need. This is your time of need. When you come back here tomorrow I will have arranged for you to pick up two one-way airline tickets to Ciudad Juarez. The flight is around two hours and forty-five minutes long. As I mentioned before, you will have to get off the plane and either walk or catch a taxi to cross the border back into the United States. When you get across the border and get to the airport in El Paso, Texas, you should go to the Continental Airlines desk, right? Isn't that the airline you flew into El Paso on?"

"Yes," said Debra.

"Go to Continental and request a lost ticket refund application. Show them the forms I typed up for you. That should be adequate information for them to issue another ticket for each of you to board the airplane and fly back to Denver, Colorado."

"Correct," said Matthew.

"I hope to see you in the morning around nine."

Then Debra asked, "Could you suggest a nearby hotel. An inexpensive hotel?"

"But, of course," he said as he opened yet another drawer in his large desk and pulled out a full-sized sheet of paper headed "INEXPENSIVE HOTELS, MEXICO CITY."

"This is what you need," he said with a wide grin on his face. "Like I said before, this is why we are here, to help out our fellow Americans."

Quickly scanning the list of hotels with Debra, Matthew asked, "Is there a pay phone we might use here in the building?"

"Yes. I'll show you where it is," said the consul. He then led them out onto the second-floor landing and to a small, fine old hardwood table with two comfortable chairs and a traditional black rotary dial phone. "There is no charge since you are making a local call."

Scanning the list for an inexpensive room, the couple called a hotel by the name of Hotel María Cristina and asked about availability and prices. When they were informed that they would have no problem getting a room and that the hotel had its own dining room, they asked for directions to the hotel from the embassy and, upon receiving them, hung up.

So down the stairs they went, and as they exited the embassy building, Matthew was especially pleased to see that there was a new guard at the gate who offered up a "Buenos días" as he and Debra left the embassy grounds and headed to the hotel some ten blocks south of the American Embassy. When they arrived, they asked for a second-floor room and were given one with no problem. They paid the front desk clerk, took their key, and headed for the stairs, bypassing the elevator as they usually did in favor of more leg work on the stairs.

The room was small but had a queen-sized bed that was decently firm. Carrying very little luggage, it took them no time to unpack. It was now late afternoon as the visit to the embassy had been a lengthy ordeal. So they decided to walk around the city partially to get some exercise and partially to unwind a bit. They felt a lot better about their situation after their visit with Mr. Davis. After walking and talking for an hour or so , but seeing very little of Mexico City as they were so focused on the events of the coming days they noticed that it was starting to get dark. They headed back to their hotel and walked into the dining room where they expected to find other people, but they were surprised to see that they were the only patrons in the room. A host sat them at a table for two and handed them each a menu, while a very young man started to fill their water glasses. Debra covered her glass with her hand and said, "No, gracias. Me gustaría una botella de agua, por favor."

"Lo siento, no," said the busboy.

"Oh," and looking at Matthew, who now understood where she was going with her inquiry about bottled water because they were warned not to drink anything in Mexico that they didn't open, she asked to see the wine and beer menu. Since they were still the only patrons in the dining room, their host-turned-waiter, having overheard the request, came over to the table and handed them the liquor menu.

"I'll take a Corona."

"Make that two Coronas, por favor," said Matthew.

They looked over the food menu, paying particular attention to the prices, and decided to get just one meal and two plates. They figured they could afford to pay for one dinner with a side of salad and a couple of bottles of beer. The look on the waiter's face was too obvious. He was waiting on the only two people in the dining room, hoping for at least one good tip, and Matthew orders one dinner, two beers, and asks if the waiter would bring two plates. Almost snatching the menus back and jamming his pen back into his shirt pocket, having not even bothered to write down their order, the waiter left the room. Maybe ten minutes later, the order showed up and Matthew and Debra consumed it in less time than it took to prepare. There they were in an almost empty dining room with the host and now one waiter whispering to one another over by the kitchen doorway, and a bus person basically standing next to an empty bus cart with his hands behind his back staring at nothing in particular while Debra and Matthew made small talk. The only noise to be heard in the room was the occasional clinking of their forks on the plates. As they finished their meal and beers, they cringed as their waiter came over. He picked up their plates and asked in English, "Would you care to see the dessert menu?"

The couple looked sheepishly at the poor man, and Debra said, "No, gracias. Could we have our check, por favor?"

Paying their meager bill but leaving a nice tip, the couple hustled out of the dining room too embarrassed to look back.

Ciudad Juarez Airport

IN THE MORNING THEY were up and out of the hotel before anyone from the hotel staff was around. They were anxious to leave their two-star hotel, but more than that, they were excited about the prospect of being back in the United States by day's end. It was to be another day filled with high hopes, nervous moments, great anxiety, and yet another rescue by some strangers.

Arriving at the US Embassy at the appointed time, the tourists from Breckenridge, Colorado, met with not Mr. Davis, but his assistant, a Mr. Dong, who initially had trouble locating the airline tickets. Just then Mr. Davis showed up having completed a short meeting with some of the other embassy staff. Mr. Dong apologized to his boss that he hadn't been able to find the airline tickets but he had found out that they had been processed and were somewhere in the building.

"No, it is I who should be apologizing. I misinformed you earlier when I told you that would find them in an AeroMexico envelope sitting in the in-box on my desk. That was not where I actually put them. I put them in the long middle drawer of my desk, probably subconsciously thinking that they would be safer out of sight."

They all moved into his office where Mr. Davis opened the top middle drawer, pulled out the AeroMexico envelope, and handed it to Debra. Of course, it was in the desk drawer. All the important items were in Mr. Davis's desk drawers.

"Thank you so much for the tickets. Now we won't have to deal with the airport ticket sales personnel. Also, we want to return the

$125 you lent us yesterday because we figured out that we would be better off just getting by on what little money we have left rather than spending the embassy money and having to pay it back who knows when." Debra then handed the $125 and the IOU back to Mr. Davis and requested that he sign it and indicate that it had been repaid. He smiled and immediately wrote PAID, dated and initialed it, and handed it to Debra. She could tell that he appreciated her way of thinking.

More than ready to get going, they said good-bye and hustled out of the embassy and onto the street where it wasn't too long before they spotted and hailed a taxi, which wasn't very hard to do because they looked just like the ones in the States—bright yellow with TAXI boldly printed on the front doors! How convenient. In about a half an hour they walked into the airport and looked up at the overhead flight board to check to see whether or not their flight, AeroMexico flight 220, was indeed there and still scheduled to leave when their tickets indicated: 18:50. It was.

It was to be a long day of sitting and people watching, reading, wandering about the airport, and, of course, napping. Eventually, 6:50 PM arrived, and they were among the first ones in line to board the plane. They easily found their seats halfway back in the twin-engine DC-3. Neither Debra nor Matthew did a lot of flying, so they sat back and thoroughly enjoyed the view, especially of the setting sun. They were getting closer to ending their ordeal in Mexico.

The flight took less than three hours, which put them into the Ciudad Juarez airport around 9:30 PM. They departed the plane and got in a line leading into a small airport terminal where once again there were the government soldiers standing both inside and outside of the terminal entrance with their rifles and sidearms, eyeing everyone. They were checking everyone's papers. Debra and Matthew were holding on tightly to their envelopes addressed to INS OFFICER IN CHARGE PORT OF ENTRY. They gave a quick glance and a tilt of the head to each other as a way of saying, "Well, here we go." By then, Matthew was taking deep breaths while trying to look as innocent of any wrong doing as possible. Debra was doing the same.

"Pasaporte o visa," said the rather chubby guard whose uniform buttons strained to hold the two halves of his shirt together.

Matthew said, "We have no passports or visas. They we stolen, but we do have these documents from the US Embassy," as both he and Debra extended their envelopes to the customs guard.

"No, no," replied the guard, rejecting the papers with the universal hand signal to stop. "Déjame ver pasaporte o visa."

Because she was far better at speaking Spanish than Matthew, Debra stepped slightly ahead of Matthew and tried her luck, "No tenemos pasaportes o visas. Fueron robados," she said while removing from the envelope the embassy document and extending it forward to the guard. Matthew did the same. "Aquí, léelo."

This time the guard actually pushed the papers away as he again demanded passports. "Pasaporte!"

Meanwhile, the people in the line behind the tourists from Colorado were getting restless. Another guard with his rifle held in both hands, in the "present arms" position as it was called in the military, had moved over closer to the scene of commotion, sensing possible trouble. Suddenly, the first guard grabbed the papers and demanded the couple to move out of the line. "Quedarse aquí!" he commanded while motioning for them to move out of the line over to a wall. Matthew and Debra did as they were told, but not without great alarm as they watched their papers leaving the room in the hands of the soldier. Fortunately, the soldier with their papers went directly into an office with windows that faced the people in line, and they were therefore able to watch as the papers were handed to what appeared to be a superior officer who read both papers and then looked out of his office at the visa-less Americans while carrying on a conversation with his subordinate border guard. Time seemed to slow to a crawl as Debra and Matthew waited and watched what was happening in the very next room. The anxiety level they were experiencing continued to climb as their heartbeats elevated.

"Do you think they are familiar with US Embassy documents?" Matthew asked Debra. "Do they notice the seal or even recognize official documents of the United States Embassy?"

"I sure hope so," responded Debra. "Surely our situation is not unique."

Then time seemed to speed up as the soldier at the desk handed the papers back. The guard came back to the couple and in a rather perturbed voice said, "Siga adelante," while motioning with the business end of his automatic weapon for them to pass on through the doorway.

"We need those papers, por favor," suggested Matthew while pointing to the two embassy documents which the guard was still clutching. Just as Matthew and Debra had done so many times during their weeks in Mexico, the guard used the visual clues to help interpret the spoken words and figure out the intended meaning. He handed the papers back to Matthew. Securing the papers and latching on to Debra's hand, he hurried them both through the small terminal and back out into the night.

Crossing the Border

THANK YOU, THANK YOU, thank you, Mr. Davis, thought Matthew as he and Debra scanned the unfamiliar surroundings outside the terminal of the airport looking for some signage that would direct them to the actual border crossing. Seeing nothing, they decided to ask someone.

"Let's find someone who looks like they know what they're doing," suggested Debra.

Just then a female and her companion who were pulling two carts overloaded with duffle bags called out to Debra and Matthew. "Hi. You two look sort of lost. Can we help you?"

"Why yes," responded Debra. "Could you help us find the easiest way to the US border crossing?"

"Sure," said the obviously American couple in unison. "We're headed there ourselves. Would you like to follow us?"

"Yes, that would be great," answered Debra.

"Do you think you could help us get our carts to a taxi?" said the female who was dressed in a fine looking traditional Mexican blouse and full-length skirt which barely revealed her leather *huaraches.*

"We'd be glad to help," said Matthew, sensing that these were exactly the kind of people that he and Debra needed to guide them out of Mexico and back to the safety of the United States. As the nearly broke couple began to assist with the carts, Debra casually asked what it was that was in the bags.

"Cloth, fine cloth from Mexico and Central America. We bring cloth to the United States and sell it to clothing makers and fabric shops in the Southwest. We're in the import business."

"That's cool," replied Debra. "Is it very profitable?"

"Oh, somewhat," replied the young man dressed in a handsome Mexican long-sleeved shirt, blue jeans, and open-toed sandals. "We do all right, but what we like about our business perhaps more than making money is that we get to travel to some really neat places and eat really good food that is not very expensive. Plus we can write off most of that as work-related expenses. How about you guys, are you here in Mexico for fun or profit or both?"

"Well, we came to have fun, but that all changed a couple of weeks ago when we got robbed on the beach."

"No kidding! That's a bummer. So, what happened?" asked the young lady.

As they made their way to the taxis, Debra shared their story of the fateful night on the beach at Zipolite. The importers were spellbound by the tale, not saying a word but letting out brief gasps of minor shock accompanied by horrified looks as Debra took them through the previous weeks' events with Matthew adding his commentary along the way.

"I am so sorry you had such a terrible experience here in Mexico," said the young lady as they arrived at the taxi station and approached a smiling cabbie. Looking at her partner, she compassionately offered to let Matthew and Debra share their taxi ride across the border. "We will pay for the taxi. Okay?"

Turning to Debra, shrugging his shoulders and raising his eyebrows simultaneously, Matthew said, "Sure, that would be great!"

Noticing that the taxi had a luggage rack, Matthew offered to load the bags onto it. Meanwhile, the young man and woman placed their personal bags and the one backpack that Debra and Matthew still had into the trunk. Once inside the taxi, the young woman offered the Colorado couple some reassuring advice.

"When we get to the border, just be calm. There will be several guards, one of which will come to the driver and ask a few questions like where we are going and what we are carrying. There will also be one or two other soldiers walking around the vehicle checking things out as well as opening up the trunk and inspecting its contents."

Now the young woman casually asked, "You guys aren't carrying anything illegal out of Mexico, are you?"

The question struck Matthew as ironic; he immediately thought of the ever-so-close call that he and Debra had had on their bus ride weeks earlier.

"Oh, uh no," said Matthew, regaining his focus to answer her question. Later that evening, it would occur to him that maybe accepting a ride with two Americans who were "importing bags of cloth" into the United States from Mexico might have been extremely foolish. Perhaps he should have asked them the same question in return.

"Good," she replied as she helped secure the bags on the luggage rack. "Now, the other thing to remember is to not look the soldiers in the eyes. They will come right up to your window and look in. You don't have to roll your window down or anything like that. Just let them look. Just don't look back at them. Just look around them if you look at all. They are looking for the nervous and or guilty look. Do you know what I mean?"

"Yes," said Matthew, nodding his head.

"Yes," said Debra.

"We'll do all the talking. We speak fluent Spanish, and we know how to handle the border guards. We don't let them bully us. We'll be fine," said the young woman.

With all that assurance, Debra and Matthew relaxed somewhat as the taxi left the airport. They were sitting side by side in the backseat with the young woman seated behind the taxi driver, Debra in the middle, and Matthew on the right side. Matthew reached for the window crank and gave it a touch-turn just to make sure it was completely closed. It was more of a symbolic action than anything as he thought about the possibility of having to engage a Spanish-speaking border guard through the window of the taxi. Perhaps a shut window would deter any guard from speaking to him.

In no time at the taxi slowed down to enter the far-right lane of four lanes at the Mexico–USA border check point. Technically, they were in Juarez, Mexico, and would be crossing into El Paso, Texas. While the north to south lanes barely slowed at the crossing, the south to north lanes were always much slower to pass through to the United States. The taxi began to move at a crawl. There was silence in the taxi, which added to the internal angst both Debra and Matthew shared but dared not speak about to one another nor to the new strangers with whom they shared the taxi, and certainly not with the Mexican taxi driver. They would share later that night that they had been thinking the identical thought and that thought, or actually wish, was that nothing else would go wrong and that they would make it through the border crossing without incident. Their nerves were about frazzled as the taxi pulled up to within a single vehicle of the checkpoint, and there they were again—armed guards in uniforms with rifles and sidearms. The importers began some small talk and then suddenly remembered that they had some fruit which past experience had taught them would be confiscated, and so they quickly decided to share a banana. They also had two apples which they offered to Matthew and Debra, but both declined the apples saying they were too nervous to eat anything.

"They will just trash any fruit that they confiscate from you. It is such a waste," said the import man as he devoured his share of the ripe banana.

"Perhaps they take the fruit home and at least feed it to their pigs or something," said his companion as the taxi crept forward.

The taxi cab's forward progress slowed to the pace of a snail as everyone in the taxi watched two guards at the checkpoint actually doing their jobs. One was conversing with the driver of the car at the checkpoint while the other guard was walking around the vehicle. It was a small four-door, white in color, but badly in need of a wash. The guard peered into each window and the trunk, which he lifted suspiciously with the barrel of his semiautomatic rifle. Meanwhile there were five or six other guards who seemed to not be doing anything other than walking around. One of them had a German shepherd, muzzled and on a leash.

Matthew could feel his palms getting wet. He had been taking deep breaths subconsciously but began to concentrate on his breathing, taking air in through his nostrils with his lips closed, then exhaling ever so quietly through pursed lips. He focused on the white car as it finally pulled away, and felt the taxi move respectfully forward and stop on a big yellow stripe painted on the pavement, perhaps two feet wide and twelve feet long. *Here we go*, thought Matthew. *Breathe easy, don't make eye contact, and everything will be alright.*

"Buenas noches," said the taxi driver as he cranked down the window by hand.

"What are you carrying?" said the guard in his well-practiced authoritarian voice as he eyed the duffle bags stacked on the roof of the taxi.

Leaning forward and slightly toward the driver so he could see the border guard, the young man said, "Cloth. Pano. Estamos llevando la tela a los mercados."

Looking back at the taxi driver, the first guard instructed him to shut off the engine and open the trunk. Understanding the routine from countless trips through customs before, the taxi driver stopped the engine, pulled the keys from the car's ignition, and opened the driver's side door, which emitted a creaky groan indicating old age. Then the driver moved to the trunk, inserted a separate key into the key slot just under the license plate, and lifted the trunk door to allow the contents to be inspected. The driver remained there holding up the trunk door as it no longer held itself up.

Meanwhile the other guard began doing his thing, which was walking around the taxi poking and prodding the bags in the luggage rack. Matthew and Debra sat motionless, looking forward, and trying to look the innocent part. But, just as the guard got to the rear right car door, he tapped on the window with the tip of his rifle. Matthew, despite being forewarned to avoid any eye contact, shot a glance at the guard. *Oh, no*, he thought, *here we go*. But the guard simply gave Matthew a toothy grin and continued poking the bags in the luggage rack. Then he moved to the rear of the taxi and peered into the trunk that the taxi driver was still holding open. Matthew guessed that the guard was just messing with him. *He probably does that a dozen times a day just to get a rise out of people*, thought Matthew.

Time seemed to be frozen for the anxious couple.

"Siga adelante," said the first guard.

The taxi driver dropped the trunk door, returned to the driver's seat, which had a rather large rip running from front to back right down the middle, inserted the ignition key, and just as he had cautiously driven up to the yellow line, drove away slowly, taking Matthew and Debra to freedom—back to the good old USA.

Back in the USA

THE FEELINGS A PERSON gets when they are set free are personal and yet universal at the same time. The fear of not knowing one's fate tends to constrict the muscles of the body including the ones surrounding the lungs. Perhaps the feeling that is most common to those who are set free is that suddenly it is easier to breathe. Matthew and Debra inhaled deeply, smiled at one another, and exhaled with immense relief.

Spotting a motel with a vacancy sign, Debra asked the driver to pull in. By then it didn't matter where they ended up just as long as it was a place to sleep in the United States.

As the young man in the front seat spoke with the driver explaining where he and his girlfriend needed to go Matthew reached over the seat and gave the driver three dollars as a tip which he figured wasn't much, but it was as much as he felt he could spare knowing that he and Debra still needed to pay for a room for the night and a meal or two before catching yet another taxi ride to the airport in the morning. He had remembered that the importers had offered to pay for the taxi, but Debra had urged him to give the driver a few extra dollars for a tip.

"Muchas gracias, señor!" exclaimed the driver.

Perhaps it was a big tip after all. Then Matthew and Debra thanked the import couple for all they had done in the past few hours and for the taxi fare. "Good luck with your business," added Debra.

"You are both very welcome and thank you for helping us with our baggage. Good luck getting back to Colorado tomorrow." And off into the night went the taxi.

The weary couple walked into the motel, asked for a double bed, and, being told that they could have room number 4 which had a double bed, they quickly checked in and made their way to the room. As they checked out the bathroom and turned on the air conditioner to make sure that it worked—it did but made a mild racket—they realized how hungry they were having not had an appetite for much of the day and evening because of the anxiety about getting out of Mexico. They closed the motel door behind them and headed hastily next door to a brightly lit, friendly looking diner that Matthew had noticed as they were checking in to the motel.

"I'm going to order the most American meal I can think of," said Matthew as he and Debra took opposite seats in a booth with bright red cushioned benches.

"Do you have apple pie?" Matthew asked the waitress who had come over to their table shortly after they had seated themselves. There were only two other customers in the diner, one of whom might have been the boyfriend or husband of the middle-aged African American waitress who was wearing an all-white over-the-knee-length dress, white shoes, and a little white half-hat.

"Yes, we do," said the waitress.

"Would you make it à la mode, please?"

"Sure. And you, miss?"

"I'll have the same," said Debra. "Could we also get some water?"

"Coming right up."

As they waited for their pie, they began to feel the intensity of the day beginning to slip away. It was like letting a heavy winter coat slide off one's shoulders after coming inside from a winter's day.

The waitress brought their order and slid the warm plates next to the napkin-wrapped knife, spoon, and fork. Matthew leaned forward to catch a whiff of the apple pie while at the same time putting both hands around the plate to receive a double dose of pleasure. The vanilla ice cream was just starting to melt and flow like lava over the brown crust of the pie and onto the warm plate where it spread out freely with nothing to stop it until Matthew took a spoon from inside the white napkin roll and scooped it up and put it into his mouth. Next came a spoonful of apple pie—not too hot, not too cold. Perfect. It was as if the waitress knew all the trials and tribulations that they had recently been through and was trying to make it all alright. At the moment it was working. Glancing up at Debra, he could tell she was also feeling much better. They smiled at one another as the only sound to be heard was the waitress clearing a cup and saucer from the diner countertop. *What a fine welcome home*, he thought.

Epilogue

FOUR YEARS LATER MATTHEW and Debra were living in Ridgway, Colorado, with their first child, Jared, who was three. To make a living, Matthew was working odd jobs. For a couple of days during the spring of 1984, Matthew was helping a local rancher clear his irrigation ditches of debris prior to the release of irrigation water. To make time pass more quickly when performing menial labor, workers tell stories. Mr. Hudson, the rancher whom Matthew was working for, was a hard worker, and he expected his crew of helpers—there were three—to keep pace with him. He didn't mind idle chatter as long as his help kept up with the ditch work. Matthew had been listening to one of the other guy's stories when he was reminded of and began to tell his story of his adventures in Mexico in 1980.

When he got to the part about Gloria, the owner of Casa de Gloria, Mr. Hudson interrupted to say that he had knowledge of Gloria and her resort in Zipolite.

"No wonder you kept running into federales. They were probably ordered by the state to keep an eye out for illegal activities like gun smuggling and drugs," said Mr. Hudson. "Gloria was running guns for the opposition."

By the opposition he meant the drug cartels, most notably the Cartel de Oaxaca, one of the smaller cartels operating in southern Mexico in the 70s and early 80s that focused then on marijuana and cocaine trafficking. As with all illegal activities, there was the need for "protecting one's interest" and that was done with guns. Allegedly, Gloria was using her hotel as a front for gun runners who moved weapons under the guise of night from speedboats to her Casa de Gloria and then most likely on inland to who knows where.

"Well, I'll be," said Matthew in disbelief. "I had no idea that such things were going on. I guess we were pretty naive as to what sorts of activities went on outside our idyllic world here in the mountain town of Ridgway, Colorado."

As they had promised Gloria that they would repay her for her food and lodging of several weeks, Matthew and Debra sent a money order for one hundred dollars (their bill for food and lodging at Casa de Gloria was 1,815 pesos or around $95) not just once but twice to Casa de Gloria. Each time the envelope was sent back, once in September of 1980 and again in October of that year. Both times they found the money order still in the envelope, and so after a time they gave up on the idea of repaying Gloria and instead cashed in the money order. They never did try to contact Gloria again.

In December of 1980, Matthew and Debra were married on the winter solstice and are still married as of this writing.

Winter, 2021

www.ingramcontent.com/pod-product-compliance
Lightning Source LLC
Chambersburg PA
CBHW071928120726
48001CB00005B/1921